What It Takes to Become a Chess Master

Andrew Soltis

BATSFORD

First published in the United Kingdom in 2012 by

Batsford
10 Southcombe Street
London
W12 0RA

An imprint of Anova Books Company Ltd

ISBN 9781849940269

A CIP catalogue record for this book is available from the British Library.

21 20 19 18 17 16 15 14 13 12
10 9 8 7 6 5 4 3 2 1

Reproduction by Rival Colour Ltd, UK

Printed and bound by Bell & Bain, Glasgow

This book can be ordered direct from the publisher at the website www.anovabooks.com, or try your local bookshop

Contents

Introduction

Only a tiny fraction of people who play chess become masters. In fact, only two percent of the people who take chess *seriously* make master. Why?

Or, to put it personally: *You* take chess seriously. You read and reread books and magazines. You may have acquired a large collection of books and/or software. You scan the Web sites that helped you get to where you are. But it doesn't seem to help you get further, to master. Why?

The answers aren't mysterious. The main reason is that the skills and know-how that helped you get this far – such as tactical sight, awareness of general principles and knowledge of basic endgame positions – have almost nothing to do with making progress to the master level.

Sure, being good in these core areas is necessary to get to where you are. But becoming better in them – going from good at tactics to great at tactics, for example – doesn't translate into much greater strength.

It's like height in basketball. Being 6-foot-tall is virtually essential to making it as a pro. And being taller, say 6-foot-6, offers a much better chance of playing in the NBA than a mere 6-foot-1 player.

But a 6-foot-9 player isn't necessarily superior to a 6-foot-6 player. (If you don't believe me, look up a 6-foot-6 guy named Michael Jordan.)

Chess players are born with their own limitations. Some, for example, have very good memories and others don't.

You need a relatively good memory to reach average strength. But a much better memory isn't going to make you a master. There have been plenty of great players with merely good memories. Or worse. Take the case of Sammy Reshevsky.

He was a world-class player for 40 years. But he had one glaring weakness, the opening. He made book mistakes as early as the sixth move and was lost in some games by the tenth move.

Fans blamed Reshevsky's lack of study. Not true, said Pal Benko, who served as his second. "We would study openings all day," Benko sighed in his memoirs. "And by evening he wouldn't remember anything we looked at."

Another ability you needed to get to where you are is calculating skill, to see at least two or three moves ahead. Many amateurs think that if they learn to calculate better, they'd play at master strength.

Well, it certainly doesn't hurt to be able to see one move further than you do now. But there's a powerful law of diminishing returns in chess calculation, just as there is in basketball height. The human who can see two moves ahead has an enormous advantage over the human who can see only one move. But being able to see, say, seven moves ahead, rather than six, is of minuscule value because you rarely have to calculate that far.

And, finally, many amateurs think that becoming a master is all about gaining 'experience.' They know that without some tournament experience they'd never have gotten as far as they are now.

True. But more experience doesn't convert into more rating points. There are players who have thousands of tournament games of experience and don't improve. On the other hand, there are 12-year-old masters who have a tiny fraction of that experience.

The Wall

The vast majority of players who take chess seriously will hit a wall: Your rating may have been steadily rising when suddenly it stops. Some players will hit the wall at about 1500 strength, others at 1700, others higher.

It's extraordinarily frustrating. Even if you reach a rating of 2100, a splendid achievement, it's just not the same as being able to call yourself a chess master.

Ed Edmondson, a longserving US Chess Federation official, helped guide Bobby Fischer to the world championship. When asked about his own strength, he said, "It depends on your point of view. The top players quite rightly consider me a 'weakie' – even though I have an expert rating and am in the top 10 percent. In this game, masters are really an exalted group."

One explanation for the wall is that most players got to where they are by learning how to not lose. When two 1700 players meet over the board, one will typically self-destruct. Not in the opening, as an 1100 player would, but by move 40, if not 30. As a result, many players can reach 1900 strength simply by not blundering.

Mastering chess takes more. It requires a new set of skills and traits. In this book I've identified nine of the attributes that are most important to making master. Some of these may be familiar to you. Others will be new.

Many of these attributes are kinds of know-how, such as understanding when to change the pawn structure or what a positionally won game looks like and how to deal with it. Some are habits, like always looking for targets. Others are refined senses, like recognizing a critical middlegame moment or feeling when time is on your side and when it isn't.

You already know the main method of acquiring these skills, traits and habits: Study master games. But that advice alone is much too vague to help anyone improve. You need more specific answers to questions like: Which games? What am I looking for when I study them? What exactly am I supposed to get from a game?

In the chapters that follow I've tried to answer some of those questions. I've suggested study techniques, study material and new approaches. These are things that typically aren't taught in books, the Internet or other obvious sources. But, after all, if it were available that way, the ranks of masters would be counted in the millions, not the thousands.

Chapter One:
What Matters Most

The biggest difference between you and a master is not his deeper opening knowledge. It is not his endgame skill. Or his ability to calculate further. The biggest difference is that he knows what he wants.

Yes, I know what you're going to say: You also know what you want. You want to deliver checkmate. We all want that.

But mate typically comes 20, 40, even 60 moves into the future of the position you're looking at. A master looks at the board and knows what kind of position he'd like to play two or three moves from now.

That's hard for non-masters to do because in any position there are so many things to weigh. There is material to count, king safety to evaluate, weak squares to consider, as well as good and bad bishops, outposts for knights, and so on.

A master can figure out what future position he wants to play because he can isolate the one or two factors that are most important: *He knows what matters most.*

Kramnik – Adams

Wijk aan Zee 2000

White to play

What do you notice when you first look at this position? Most players will start by counting material. They'll conclude White is better because he has an extra pawn.

Better players will know better. "What matters most in queen endings," they'll say, "is how close a pawn is to queening." They're right. The player with the passed pawn closest to queening usually has a big, if not decisive, edge.

But here that doesn't help much. Black's b-pawn is just as fast as either of White's pawns, as 1 ♕e7? b3 2 d6 b2 shows.

Is there something else, something that matters even more? Yes. A master will notice another feature of the position that stands out. Believe it or not, it's a diagonal.

It's the one that runs from a8 to h1. Whoever controls that diagonal controls the queening square of the a-pawn. That's a big deal.

But there's more. Next to queening the b-pawn, Black's only source of counterplay is checking the White king. The only way he can do that is if he controls the a8-h1 diagonal. For example, if White plays 1 ♕c6 Black shoots back 1 ... ♕e4+!.

White to play

If White moves his king (or plays 2 f3 ♕e2+) Black will suddenly have the winning chances following ... b3!. Plainly, 1 ♕c6? fails.

Well, then, what if White eliminates that pesky b-pawn? Then Black's counterplay will be limited to queen checks.

The way to get rid of the b-pawn is 1 a6 so that 1 ... ♕xa6 allows 2 ♕e4+ and 3 ♕xb4. Black can't avoid this by way of 1 ... b3 because after the queening race, 2 a7 b2 3 a8(♕) b1(♕), White can mate on g8 or h8.

White will probably win in the 3 ♕xb4 line. But he still has a lot of work to do after, say, 3 ... ♕a8.

Instead, White was able to end the game in a few moves with **1 d6!**. The point is that he wins control of the diagonal after 1 ... ♕xd6 2 ♕e4+! and ♕b7. For example, 2 ... g6 3 ♕b7! threatens ♕xf7+ as well as pushing the a-pawn.

Black to play

Black can resign in view of 3 ... ♔g7 4 a6 and 5 a7. Black also loses after 2 ... ♕g6 3 ♕b7 or 2 ... ♔g8 3 ♕b7. The ♕b7 idea beats all defenses. It wins because what matters most is the a8-h1 diagonal.

In the game, Black met 1 d6 with **1 ... b3**. But he was too slow in the queening race after **2 d7**, e.g. 2 ... ♕c6+ 3 ♔h2 b2 4 d8(♕) ♕xe8 5 ♕xe8 b1(♕) 6 ♕xf7 and wins.

When you realize how important that h1-a8 diagonal is, this ending goes from being incredibly difficult to fairly routine. And note how little White had to calculate.

He only had to visualize the position in the last diagram when he looked at the first one. That's just two and a half moves into the future. Anyone who aspires to be a master should be able to see that far, particularly when there are so few pieces on the board.

By figuring out what matters most, a master strips a position down to its most important elements. Let's consider a case that comes straight out of the opening.

Timman – Winants, Brussels 1988: **1 d4 ♘f6 2 c4 e6 3 ♘c3 ♗b4 4 ♗g5 h6 5 ♗h4 c5 6 d5 d6 7 e3 g5 8 ♗g3 ♘e4 9 ♕c2 ♕f6 10 ♘e2**

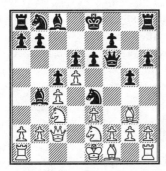

Timman – Winants

Brussels 1988

Black to play

Black chose a natural move, **10 ... exd5**. He assumed that after White recaptured, 11 cxd5, he would obtain good play with 11 ... ♗f5. The bishop move protects the e4-knight and threatens to discover an attack on the White queen (12 ... ♘xg3, 12 ... ♘xc3, 12 ... ♘xf2).

But consider the diagram a little more. What strikes you about White's position?

There are a lot of things to focus on. But White realized that what really matters is that he has a slight lead in development. Four of his pieces are out, compared with three for Black. That didn't change after 10 ... exd5 because the capture is not a developing move.

Black believed he had made a forcing move. But even in a complex position like this, development matters more. White lengthened his lead with **11 0-0-0!**.

Black to play

Castling like this is the kind of magic-move that some amateurs marvel at. But it isn't magic. It's appreciating how development trumps material once again. (Paul Morphy would have spotted 11 0-0-0! immediately.)

Because of the threat of 12 ♘xd5!, Black has no time for 11 ... ♗f5, not to mention 11 ... ♘xf2. He chose to get rid of the White knights, **11 ... ♗xc3 12 ♘xc3 ♘xc3**.

But White tipped the ratio of developed pieces further in his favor with **13 ♕xc3!**. Black didn't have a good alternative (13 ... d4 14 exd4 ♘c6 15 ♕e3+!) so he went reluctantly into the endgame, **13 ... ♕xc3+ 14 bxc3**.

He would have been in bad shape after 14 ... ♔e7 in view of 15 h4! g4 16 ♖xd5 ♖d8 17 ♖h5. But what he played was worse, **14 ... dxc4 15 ♗xc4**.

Black to play

This truly strips the position down to its most important elements. All the extraneous factors are gone.

Black will lose the d6-pawn and material will become equal. But White's active pieces, particularly the two bishops, confer a huge edge. He has a choice of strong continuations, e.g. 15 ... ♘c6 and now 16 ♗xd6 b6 17 ♖d2 and ♖hd1 or 16 ♖xd6 and 17 ♖hd1 are both strong.

The game actually went **15 ... &e6 16 &xe6 fxe6 17 &xd6 &e7 18 &hd1 &f6** and now **19 f4! 公c6 20 fxg5+ hxg5 21 &d7! b6 22 &f1+ &g6 23 &d6 公d8 24 &e5! resigns** (in view of 24 ... &e8 25 g4! and 26 &f6+).

Do's and Don'ts

Figuring out what matters most is hard. What makes it hard is that from our first days of studying chess we are bombarded with do's and don'ts.

At first, these tips seem like a godsend. They give you a way to evaluate positions. You decide to advance a knight because you were told the value of outposts. You shift a rook because you read about how good it is to control an open file.

But after you've digested another bushel or two of do's and don'ts you realize that some conflict with others. You can't obey all of them in the same position. As a result, you can find yourself more confused than you were before you had any advice. This is painfully clear in the games of some novices who talk themselves out of winning a knight because it would mean doubling their pawns.

Here's how a master puts pawn structure in perspective.

Anand – Kasparov

World Championship
match 1995

Black to play

On general principles Black has to be wary of putting his attacked knight offside at h5 or g4. The natural reply is 1 ... 公fd5 and then 2 公xd5 公xd5.

But that leaves White with a free hand to attack the kingside, which now has only one defensive piece, the bishop at e7. Black might have to worry about an immediate, forcing line, perhaps, 3 公g5 &xg5 4 &h5, which threatens &xh7+ and &xf7+/&xd7 as well as &xg5.

However, Garry Kasparov solved Black's kingside problems with virtually no calculation. He replied **1 ... 公fd5 2 公xd5 exd5!**.

White to play

He reasoned that White's bishop at d3 was his most dangerous weapon: No bishop, no attack. The go-for-mate line 3 ♘g5 ♗xg5 4 ♕h5 now fails to 4 ... ♘xd3!.

True, 2 ... exd5 sticks Black with an isolated pawn. But that pawn is much less significant than a kingside attack.

White was forced to look for another way to win. He chose **3 ♖e1 h6 4 c3 ♘xd3 5 ♕xd3**.

He was aiming for a positional edge. A well-placed White knight can dominate Black's bad light-squared bishop. That can be an important, even winning advantage in the hands of a good player.

Black to play

But Black understood that what mattered most is whether the knight gets to d4. If it does, it severely restricts the bishop at d7. If it doesn't, the knight isn't a big factor.

Once you realize this, it's easier to find **5 ... ♗c5**. General principles tell us that the player with the two bishops should not trade one of them. But 5 ... ♗c5! stops the knight from enjoying his ideal outpost because 6 ♗xc5 ♖xc5 7 ♘d4? ♖xe5 just drops a pawn.

Instead, White played **6 ♕xd5** but Black had foreseen that **6 ... ♗e6** would be good for him. After **7 ♕d2 ♗xb6 8 axb6 ♖c6** the b6-pawn is lost. The game was drawn soon afterwards. Black had twice passed the 'what matters' test.

Bobby Fischer gave the highest praise to young players who had a clear idea of their goals in a position. When he saw 16-year-old Ken Rogoff for the first time, Fischer said what impressed him the most "was his self-assured style and his knowing exactly what he wanted over the chessboard."

What White wanted in the next example changed significantly from move to move. That can happen even in a quiet position.

Sorokin – Belikov
Russian Championship
1995

Black to play

Black has spent several tempi in the opening to get his pieces to protect the pawn at d4 (that knight on c6 came from g8!).

White, in turn, played c2-c3 to tempt 1 ... dxc3. Then 2 bxc3 would allow him to control d4 with a pawn. If he can follow up with d3-d4!, he gains important space and shuts out Black's bishop.

So, Black played the consistent **1 ... ♕b6**, which overprotects d4 and threatens 2 ... dxc3 and 3 ... ♗xf2+.

White shot back **2 c4!**. At first this looks inconsistent and ugly: It surrenders the fight for d4 and makes his bishop on b3 into nothing more than a big pawn.

But White appreciated that 2 c4! renders Black's bishop and queen toothless. It also means there is only one obvious target left on the board and it's a big one, the Black kingside. After **2 ... d6 3 ♕g4!** 0-0, White obtains dangerous play with 4 cxb5 axb5 5 ♘f3, threatening 6 ♗h6.

Black preferred **3 ... g6** and then came **4 cxb5 axb5 5 ♘f3**.

Black to play

13

Black has won the battle for d4. But that square has become virtually meaningless. White's attack is what matters most.

With ♗h6 or ♗g5-f6 coming up, Black was in major trouble. The rest was **5 ... h6 6 ♕h4 ♕d8? 7 ♗g5 ♕b6 8 ♗f6 ♖f8 9 ♕xh6 ♗a6 10 ♘g5 ♘e5 11 ♕g7 resigns**.

Throughout history, masters have changed the way we play this game by pointing out new ways to appreciate 'what matters most'. F.A.Philidor explained how pawns, not pieces, could be the most important feature in a position. Morphy showed us how development can matter most in open positions. Wilhelm Steinitz stressed that positional goodies, like the two-bishop advantage, matter a lot. Fischer demonstrated why you have to give up control of certain squares in order to control others that are more important.

What today's masters appreciate is that even subtle changes in a position, made by just one or two innocuous-looking moves, can make a big difference – as long as the changes affect what matters most.

Adams – Radjabov
Enghien-les-Bains 2003

White to play

Black has weaknesses all over his side of the board. But it's hard to get at them because he also has targets to attack, at b2 and f4, and he can use the f2-b6 diagonal tactically.

For instance, if he is allowed to play 1 ... ♗c5 and 2 ♗xc5 ♕xc5+ 3 ♔f1 he has 3 ... ♕b4!, attacking the f- and b-pawns.

White can avert that with 1 ♗c4 and then 1 ... ♗c5 2 ♗xc5 ♕xc5+ 3 ♔f1. But 3 ... ♕f5 is annoying.

It stands to reason that if tactics are the problem White should take steps to eliminate them. He began with the unassuming **1 ♔g1!**. Then came **1 ... ♗c5 2 ♗xc5+ ♕xc5+ 3 ♔h1**.

Black to play

White has played three more or less routine moves since the previous diagram. But the position is no longer double-edged. White has a serious edge.

What made the difference? Of course, it's the White king. It is now out of checking range. Once the king is no longer a factor, there's something else that matters most, the insecure Black king and pawns.

White can hammer e6 with b2-b3 and ♗c4. Or he can try to get his queen to g7 via ♕g4. Or he can look for action on the other wing with ♖ac1.

Thanks to ♔g1-h1 the previously unclear position was won by White in a few moves, **3 ... ♕b4 4 ♕e3! ♕a5** (or 4 ... ♕xb2 5 ♖ab1 and 4 ... ♕b6 5 ♕g3 ♔f7 6 b3 and ♗c4).

Black resigned after **5 b3 ♗d7 6 ♗c4 ♖bd8 7 ♖e1 ♕b6 8 ♕g3 ♖dg8 9 ♕h3** in view of 10 ♗xe6.

Priorities

All players set priorities. You do it in some positions, such as when you choose between a two-move win of a pawn or a three-move sequence that forces checkmate. Yes, the two-mover is shorter. It's easier to calculate. There's less chance of an oversight.

But it's obvious to you that the three-mover is more desirable. Mate counts more.

As you face stronger opponents on your road to masterhood, you don't get such easy choices. To break 2200, you need a more refined sense of priorities. You need to appreciate how, for example, a single misplaced piece may be decisive.

Yakovich – McShane
Stockholm 1998

White to play

White's pieces are better placed. But that can be temporary. In light of the symmetrical nature of the position, a draw is likely if Black can trade a pair, or all, of the rooks.

However, Black is not ready for ... ♖ac8 or ... ♖ad8 because either move would hang the a7-pawn. This tells us Black has to move his knight so he can play ... a6.

White appreciated how much that knight mattered. It's actually the most important feature of the position. Once you understand that, it's easier to realize how good 1 a3! and 2 b4! are.

Then the knight can't move (1 ... ♘b8 2 ♘c7). That means the a-pawn can't move. And that means the QR can't move.

After **1 a3!** Black tried **1 ... ♖fd8 2 b4! e5 3 ♘b3 ♘c4** based on 4 ♖xc4?? ♖xd1 mate. But after **4 ♔f1! ♖xd1+ 5 ♖xd1 ♔e7 6 ♔e2!** he was running out of useful moves.

Black to play

The a-pawn would fall after 6 ... ♖d8 7 ♖xd8 ♔xd8 8 ♔d3!. Black would also lose a queenside pawn after 6 ... ♘b6 7 ♘a5.

Black tried **6 ... f6**. In such a commanding position White has a choice of promising plans. One idea is 7 ♖c1. Another is 7 e4 followed by ♖d5 and ♔d3.

White preferred to create an invasion route on the kingside with **7 g4 h6 8 h4**. Black lost his patience and the game as well after **8 ... ♔e6 9 ♘c5+ ♘xc5 10 ♘c7+**.

Siegbert Tarrasch would have been pleased by that game. It validates his own views about what matters most. To Tarrasch, chess was all about piece mobility. If one piece stands badly, like Black's knight at a6, his whole game stands badly, he wrote.

But in middlegames there are lots of pieces, and this increases the likelihood that you can afford to make one bad. The sum of all the other pieces and pawns matters more.

Lanka – I. Sokolov
Batumi 1999

Black to play

The position is riddled with positional plusses and minuses: Good and bad pieces, holes and outposts, doubled pawns, pawn islands, and so on.

Black might be tempted to play 1 ... c4+, to liberate the b6-bishop, his worst piece. But he chose **1 ... d4!**, making it much worse.

One reason he did so was to open the diagonal of the other bishop. The one at b7 has a brighter future than its brother because it has targets to hit, at f3 and (after ... g4) at g2.

Another point in favor of 1 ... d4! is that White wanted to bring his knights into play, via e3. After 1 ... c4+ a White knight might also be able to occupy d4, either immediately or later.

But 1 ... d4! makes the White knights almost useless. Play continued **2 ♘a3 ♕d5 3 c4 ♕c6**.

White to play

Black might not be able to use his b6-bishop until an endgame, 30 moves away. But all his other pieces are doing their jobs in the middlegame, and that's what matters most.

His immediate plan is ... g4 and ... gxf3. But 1 ... d4! also gave Black more operating room, and that enables him to consider an alternate winning plan. He can double rooks on the e-file and win the e-pawn (4 ♕d3 ♖e7 and 5 ... ♖ae8, followed by ... ♘xg3 and ... ♖xe5).

White stopped the ... g4 push with **4 h3** so Black switched to his second plan, **4 ... ♕g6 5 ♘b5 ♖e6**.

White avoided ... ♘xg3 by playing **6 ♗h2** but **6 ... ♘f4!** shut the bishop out of play.

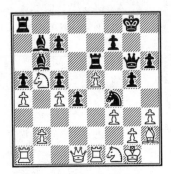

White to play

Black's b6-bishop is still a bystander. But White is losing, if not lost. This became clearer after Black doomed the e-pawn – **7 ♗xf4 gxf4 8 ♘h2 h5!** (to stop ♘g4) **9 ♕d2 ♕f5 10 ♖e2 ♖ae8**.

The e-pawn fell with **11 ♖ae1 ♖xe5 12 ♖xe5 ♖xe5 13 ♖xe5 ♕xe5**. However the ultimate humiliation was that White's knights remained useless while he was done in by the resurrected b6-bishop.

The finish was **14 ♘f1 ♗c8 15 ♔f2 c6! 16 ♘a3 ♗d8! 17 ♔g1 ♗f5 18 b3 ♗h4 19 ♕d1 ♕e1! 20 ♕d2 ♗g3! White resigns**. After 21 ♕xe1 ♗xe1 and ... ♗b4, it is White's QN that proves to be the worst piece on the board.

Prioritizing Practice

A good way to develop and refine your sense of what matters most is to examine early middlegame positions from master games. Your aim is to figure out what are White's priorities, what are Black's and why some changes in the position will favor one side significantly. If a position in an annotated game changes from unclear or even at move 15 to a plus-over-equals at move 20 or 25, try to figure out what changed. That will likely tell you what mattered most.

One approach is to focus on middlegames that arise from opening variations that are new to you, ones you've never played or studied before. A Catalan Gambit or one of the sacrificial lines of the Queen's Indian Defense may be useful for a 1 e4 player, for example.

For the sake of introduction, let's consider some Sicilian Defense middlegames, beginning with one from the game Sanikidze – Kacheishvilli, Georgian Championship 2004: **1 e4 c5 2 ♘f3 d6 3 d4 cxd4 4 ♘xd4 ♘f6 5 ♘c3 ♘c6 6 f3 e5 7 ♘b3 ♗e7 8 ♗e3 0-0 9 ♕d2 a5 10 ♗b5 ♗e6 11 0-0-0 ♘e8 12 g4 ♘c7 13 ♔b1 ♕b8 14 ♗b6 ♖c8 15 ♗a4**

**Sanikidze –
Kacheishvili**
Georgian Championship
2004

Black to play

Black carried out an unusual maneuver of his knight to c7 and put his queen on the unlikely square of b8. Meanwhile, instead of attacking the king, White piled up his pieces on the queenside and made the rare move ♗b6. What's going on?

If you consider this for a while you may be able to see that there's a below-the-radar battle. Black is trying hard to play a move and White seems almost desperate to stop that move from happening.

Which move could be that important? It shouldn't be difficult to figure it out. It's ... b5.

If Black cannot push his b-pawn, his queenside attack is halted. White would have a free hand to advance his pawns to g5 and h5 and break open Black's king position. This is why spending time on prophylactic moves can win time for you later, as we'll see in Chapter Five. Here White would get an edge after 15 ... ♘b4 16 h4 ♘7a6 17 a3 ♘c6 18 ♘d5! for example.

Once you appreciate how much ... b5 matters, the next few moves of the game begin to make sense: **15 ... ♖a6! 16 ♕f2 ♘a8! 17 ♗e3 ♘c7 18 ♗b6! ♘a7! 19 ♘c1 ♘a8! 20 ♗e3 b5!**.

White to play

White's blockade on b6 is broken. His kingside attack never got past g2-g4. Both of these factors freed Black to take charge after **21 ♗b3 a4 22 ♗xe6 fxe6 23 ♘3e2 b4 24 f4 ♘b5!**.

There are a lot of clever tactical points from here on. But what you should appreciate is that the game became one-sided once White lost the battle over ... b5. There followed **25 fxe5 ♘c3+! 26 ♘xc3 bxc3 27 b3 axb3 28 ♘xb3 ♛b4!**.

White can't stop the queen from reaching a4 or a3, and the game ended with **29 ♗c1 ♛a4 30 a3 dxe5 31 ♖hf1 ♗xa3 32 ♗h6!? ♖a7! 33 ♗e3 ♗c5! 34 ♖d3 ♛a2+ 35 ♔c1 ♛a1+! White resigns** in view of **36 ♘xa1 ♖xa1 mate**.

Okay, that wasn't too hard, at least once you figure out how big a deal ... b5 was. Let's move on to another Sicilian position, a quite a bit different one, from the game Kasimdzhanov – Anand, Linares 2005:

1 e4 c5 2 ♘f3 d6 3 c3 ♘f6 4 ♗e2 ♗g4 5 d3 e6 6 ♘bd2 ♘c6 7 ♘f1 d5 8 exd5 ♘xd5 9 ♛a4 ♗h5 10 ♘g3 ♘b6 11 ♛d1 ♗g6 12 0-0 ♗e7 13 a4 0-0 14 a5 ♘d5 15 ♛a4 ♛c7 16 d4 cxd4 17 ♛xd4 ♘xd4 18 ♛xd4

**Kasimdzhanov –
Anand**
Linares 2005

Black to play

It's a Sicilian position that may be quite unfamiliar to a devoted Dragon or Najdorf Variation player. Once again your task is to figure out what matters most. Before reading on, take several minutes to consider what should be important to each player and which factors take precedence.

Done that? Then let's consider the plusses for White. He has a queenside majority of pawns. We can also see he has a nicely centralized queen.

But the queen can be driven away by ... ♗f6 or ... ♗c5. Or by putting a Black rook on d8 and discovering an attack along the d-file, such as ... ♘b4. And as for the queenside majority, well that might be a factor in an endgame. But as for now ...

Black appreciated that what matters most is the *kingside* majority because it is immediately useful. He played **18 ... f5!**, which prepares ... e5 with a commanding center.

This makes his bishop at g6 bad. But taking e4 away from White's g3-knight matters more. This becomes clearer after 19 ♗f3 ♖ad8 20 ♛a4 e5! and 21 ... e4.

White chose the superior **19 ♛a4 ♖ad8 20 ♖d1** so that he could meet 20 ... e5 with 21 ♗c4!, gaining counterplay on the c4-g8 diagonal.

Black to play

Black can advance his f-pawn again but that gives up control of the e4-square that he just seized. So take a few minutes before you read on and see if you can figure out what matters most.

Time's up. What matters most is White's constricted position. The way to emphasize that is **20 ... f4!** It severely limits White's bishop at c1 and thereby keeps the rook at a1 in limbo.

If White had retreated 21 ♘f1 – or even 21 ♘h1 – the overwhelming benefits of 20 ... f4! would have been obvious. White played **21 ♘e4** but **21 ... ♛e5!** was strong, e.g. 22 ♗d3? ♘xc3! loses material (23 bxc3 ♗xe4).

White chose **22 ♗f3** instead. There are several appealing responses but the best was **22 ... b5!**, based on 23 ♛xb5? ♗xe4 and 23 axb6? ♘xb6 24 ♛c2 ♗xe4 25 ♗xe4 ♛xe4!.

White had to play **23 ♛c2** and Black forced a favorable position with **23 ... ♘f6! 24 ♘xf6+ ♛xf6 25 ♛b3 ♖xd1+ 26 ♛xd1 ♖d8 27 ♛e2 ♗d3 28 ♛e1 e5**.

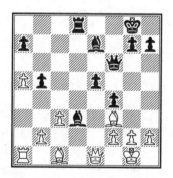

White to play

This culminates the strategy begun by 18 ... f5!. The Black center pawns are choking White. He still can't activate his queenside (29 ♗d2 e4 30 ♗xe4? ♗xe4 31 ♛xe4 ♖xd2).

Instead, he chose **29 ♗e2 ♛xe2 30 ♛xe2** and now **30 ... e4!** based on another last-rank tactic (31 ♛xe4?? ♖d1+).

The Black center pawns performed one final service, creating a mating

21

attack that ended the game soon after **31 g3 e3! 32 fxe3 f3! 33 ♕xb5 f2+ 34 ♔g2 ♖f8**, with the idea of ... f1(♕)+.

The reason that examining games like these is valuable is that it increases your knowledge of different kinds of positions. The main reason that a modern player would be superior to, say, Rudolf Spielmann or Richard Reti, or any of the great players of the early 20th century, is that today we know many, *many* more positions than a Spielmann or a Reti. We know what counts most in those positions.

This also provides one reason – there are others – for why today's masters are superior to today's amateurs. The masters know and understand more positions. Occasionally an amateur will do well against a master because he gets into one of the positions he understands well. But the master will win the majority of games from him because he'll be able to reach middlegames that the amateur doesn't know.

Let's try one final Sicilian middlegame. It comes from Short – Topalov, Novgorod 1997:

1 e4 c5 2 ♘f3 d6 3 d4 cxd4 4 ♘xd4 ♘f6 5 ♘c3 a6 6 ♗e3 ♘g4 7 ♗g5 h6 8 ♗h4 g5 9 ♗g3 ♗g7 10 ♗e2 h5 11 ♗xg4 ♗xg4 12 f3 ♗d7 13 ♗f2 ♘c6 14 0-0 e6 15 ♘xc6 ♗xc6 16 ♗d4

Short – Topalov
Novgorod 1997

Black to play

White wants to eliminate Black's two-bishop advantage and create kingside chances. The bishops and the kingside are among the most important factors in evaluating the position.

But what else matters? Once again, take several minutes to examine the diagram. See if you can determine what the two players are aiming for. Where are the weaknesses?

And specifically, how should Black answer 16 ♗d4 ? Is it worth preserving his bishop with 16 ... e5 ? After all, he does it with a gain of time. Or is the hole created on d5 more significant? And what are the worthwhile alternatives? Does Black really want to castle here?

If you've given this position the attention it deserves you may have considered the best move. It is **16 ... ♗e5!**.

Black knew from similar positions that the doubling of pawns on the e-file wasn't as important as having pawn control of d5 and d4. He pressed the point by meeting **17 ♕d2** with **17 ... ♕f6!**.

White didn't relish the prospect of going into a somewhat inferior ending after 18 ♖ad1 ♗xd4+ or 18 ... ♕f4 19 ♕xf4 gxf4.

So the game went **18 ♗xe5 dxe5!**.

White to play

Note that White has no way to open up the position further for his rooks now that f3-f4 is ruled out. Moreover, he has no obvious target to attack.

When you can't change the pawn structure favorably, you should make the most of your pieces. Here that means White should try 19 ♕d6 ♖d8 20 ♕c5.

That would prompt Black to find a way to get his king to safety and connect rooks, such as after 20 ... ♕g7 and ... f6/... ♕e7/... ♔f7. In other words, what matters in this position is the temporary discomfort of the Black pieces after 19 ♕d6!.

Instead, White slipped into the worst of it after **19 a4? 0-0 20 b3 ♖fd8 21 ♕e3** and then **21 ... ♕f4! 22 ♕xf4 gxf4!**.

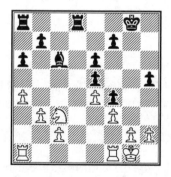

White to play

Quite a bit has changed so it's time to re-evaluate. What matters most now?

Well, White has a queenside majority of pawns and a frisky knight that can carry out a useful regrouping, such as ♘a2-b4 and then c2-c4.

Black's plusses include control of the d-file but that's temporary. He has targets at g2 and possibly f3, which could be exposed by ... f5. White went steadily downhill – **23 ♖fd1 h4 24 ♖xd8+ ♖xd8 25 ♖d1 ♖c8!**. Black preserves his rook to attack g2 and/or c2.

Then came **26 ♖d2 ♔f8 27 ♘d1 ♔e7 28 ♘f2 f5! 29 ♔f1 fxe4 30 fxe4 a5!** (to fix the queenside pawns) **31 ♔e2 ♗e8!**.

Black's bishop can join the attack in variations such as 32 c4 ♗h5+ 33 ♔f1 ♖d8 34 ♖xd8 ♔xd8 35 ♘d3 ♗d1! or 33 ♔e1 ♖d8 34 ♖xd8 ♔xd8 35 ♘d3 ♗g6.

White preferred **32 ♔d1 ♗h5+ 33 ♔c1 ♖g8 34 ♘d3 h3** but eventually lost.

Aside from examining late opening positions – which are easily found in books, magazines and databases or on the Internet – there is another good method for enriching your sense of what matters. It's your own games. Unfortunately for your ego, it's usually your losses.

The reason is that by the time you've been playing tournament chess for several years, you've developed an appreciation of what matters in some positions. But you're also hampered by blind spots in other kinds of positions. The best way to find out what you don't understand is by examining positions you didn't understand when you played them. Here's a personal example.

Huebner – Soltis
Ybbs 1968

Black to play

I had sought this pawn structure and thought I had cleverly found a way to swap some minor pieces, **1 ... ♘d4** (2 ♘xd4? exd4 3 ♕xd4 ♘xe4) so that I wouldn't be constricted.

Play continued **2 ♗e3 ♘xf3+ 3 ♕xf3** and now I figured I should get rid of my bad bishop and did so with **3 ... ♘d7 4 a4 ♗f6 5 a5 ♗g5 6 ♗xg5 ♕xg5**. I was making progress.

It was only after **7 ♘a4!** that I began to realize that I had badly misevaluated. If I move my knight – and there's no really good square for it – I allow a strong ♘b6. And if I don't move the knight, how do I develop my queenside?

I went ahead with the attack-the-base-of-the-pawn chain plan of **7 ... f5**. After all, wasn't that what all the textbooks said you did with this kind of pawn structure? There followed **8 ♕a3! ♕f6 9 exf6 gxf5 10 ♖ac1**.

Black to play

It was already too late. White will penetrate with ♖c7 (since 10 ... ♕d8 allow 11 ♕xd6).

I tried to complicate with **10 ... e4 11 f4 ♕d4+ 12 ♔h2 e3** but had to resign shortly after **13 ♖c4! ♕d2 14 ♕c3 ♕f2 15 ♗e2 ♖e4!? 15 ♖xc8+**.

Only in the post-mortem did I realize that what mattered most wasn't my having the better bishop or getting in the thematic ... f5. The hole on b6, the open c-file and other factors were much more important. The positions I had sought while choosing moves were simply ones I should have avoided.

Quiz

Now let's see if you can figure out what matters most in the following positions. There will be similar quizzes at the end of each succeeding chapter. Take your time, at least five minutes, trying to find the right answer. When you're done you'll find the correct answers at the end of this book.

1
Spraggett – Morovic
Spanish Championship
1994

White to play

What is the most important feature of the position and what should White do about it?

2
Carlsen – Anand
Linares 2009

White to play

White played 1 ♘c7. Why does that make sense?

3

White to play

In this standard opening position Black has just played ... ♘c6. Many players would be tempted to separate Black's pawns with 1 ♘xc6. But why do some masters prefer the time-losing retreat 1 ♘f3 ?

4
Anand – Shirov
Frankfurt 2000

White to play

Both players have wing attacks in motion. What should White do?

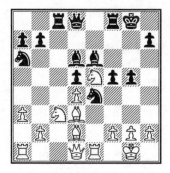

5
Fressinet – Gelfand
Cannes 2002

Black to play

Black's best bishop is clearly the one at d6. Should he even consider 1 ... ♗xe5 ?

6
Belyavsky – Mitkov
Panorma 2001

White to play

In this book position, the routine continuations were 1 ♗f4 and 1 ♗e3. Is there anything better?

Chapter Two:
Habits

Good chess comes from good habits. Making the jump to master requires taking something that you know is a good trait and turning it into a habit.

You already have several good habits. You might not appreciate them but you do. For example, when you were a beginner you were told that as soon as your opponent makes a move you should look to see whether he made a threat. At first you had to make a conscious effort to do this. But after a while you did it automatically. It had become a habit.

You already know some, if not most, of the traits that masters have made their habits. But you probably don't take them as seriously as a master does – perhaps because they sound too simple. For instance:

A master always looks for targets.

The easiest way to find the best move in a typical position is to take note of the pieces and pawns that you can attack. You might be able to attack them on the next move or on the move after that or even at some distant future point.

Gonzalez – Foisor
Balaguer 2004

White to play

Black's pieces are somewhat more active than White's and he has a passed c-pawn as well as a threat, 1 ... bxc5.

Yet White's best strategy should be to ignore all that and attack. The attack should be directed at g7. Why?

What makes g7 a target is that Black has no pieces that can easily defend it, just his king. White, on the other hand, can throw virtually all of his pieces at g7.

White began with **1 ♗g5!**. His idea was 2 ♕g4 followed by either ♗f6 or ♗h6 and ♕xg7 mate.

That's a very primitive threat. With so much material on the board it might seem that Black can parry it easily.

He can't. If he plays ... ♔h8 and ... ♖g8 to secure g7 he makes h7 another high-value target.

That's what happened in the game, which went **1 ... bxc5 2 ♕g4 ♔h8 3 ♖f3 cxd4 4 ♖h3.**

Black to play

White will play ♕h5 or ♕h4 and threaten ♕xh7 mate. He can answer ... h6 with the crushing ♗xh6.

Black tried **4 ... f5** so that 5 exf5 ♕xe5 6 ♕h4 ♕xf5 would defend. Or 5 exf6 g6 6 ♕h4 ♖f7.

But he resigned soon after **5 ♕h5! ♔g8 6 ♕xh7+ ♔f7 7 ♕h5+ ♔g8 8 ♗f6!.**

Black lost because g7 was weak and because he had no counterplay to distract White from attacking it. He needed to find his own targets. For example, 2 ... ♕c3!, instead of 2 ... ♔h8, would allow him to meet 3 ♗f6 with 3 ... ♕e3+ and 4 ... ♕h6. And on 3 ♖ad1 Black has 3 ... ♗a4!. His bishop, which can play no role in defense, can attack. The game would become very double-edged after 4 ♗h6 g6 5 ♕f4 f5!.

The moral is: White had a plan, a strong one, as soon as he recognized that g7 was a target. Black failed to recognize targets and lost.

When you were a beginner you probably got into the habit of looking at all the captures available to you when it was your turn to move. The habit of looking for targets is just an extension of this. In addition to "What can I take?" you want to ask yourself "What can I attack in a few moves?"

This sounds too simpleminded to many amateurs. Why look for enemy pieces and pawns that you can't immediately attack?

This way of thinking blinds the player to opportunities like the following.

Am. Rodriguez – Sorin
Matanzas 1993

White to play

Look for the target in Black's camp before you read any further.

See it? The only member of Black's army that is not protected is the pawn at g7. It's easy to overlook because it's shielded on the g-file by two pieces.

Of course, not every target is worth going after. But here it shouldn't be hard to grasp that if White can play ♕xg7, he's doing very well.

Once you identify a target – and determine that it's worth going after – the next step is to figure out how to get at it. There may not be a way: It's not always possible to exploit a target.

But in this case White found **1 e6!**. He threatens 2 ♕xg4, and 1 ... ♗h5 2 ♕g5 is no antidote. After the forced reply, **1 ... ♗xe6**, came **2 h4!**.

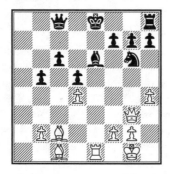

Black to play

White threatens 3 h5 and then 3 ... ♘-moves 4 ♕xg7. If Black tries to protect g7 with his king, it becomes a bigger target. For example, 2 ... 0-0 3 h5 ♘e7 4 ♗h6! g6 5 ♕e5! and wins.

Another line would be 2 ... ♔f8 3 h5 ♘e7 4 h6 g6 5 ♗g5! followed by ♕d6 and/or ♖a1-a7. And another is 2 ... ♖g8 3 f4!.

In the end, Black gave up on defending the target and lost after **2 ... ♔d7 3 h5 ♘e7 4 ♕xg7**.

Beginners often make a concerted effort to threaten their opponent's queen simply because it's so valuable. But queens are valuable because they're so mobile. They can run away. The best targets are typically pawns because they tend to be stationary. Most stationary of all are squares because, obviously, they cannot move.

But why would a square be valuable enough to become a target? Consider the next example:

Kamsky – Grischuk
Olympiad 2010

Black to play

At first Black's only target seems to be the d-pawn. But 1 ... ♖xd3 is complicated by 2 ♘e1.

An alternative is 1 ... ♖df8, which threatens 2 ... ♖xf1. Then if White moves his rook from f1, Black can play ... ♖f2 and try to exploit the knight at g2, perhaps with a ... ♘g6xh4 sacrifice.

But Black wondered what he would do after 2 ♖xf3. The recapture 2 ... ♖xf3 isn't bad. But when he evaluated 2 ... gxf3, he realized that h3 becomes a target.

With the g-pawn out of the way, Black may be able to get to h3 with his queen. That's why Black found the stunning **1 ... ♗b7!**.

It is tactically justified by 2 ♘xa7? ♖a8, pinning the doomed knight. But the main point of 1 ... ♗b7 is to continue ... ♗c8 at the moment when h3 is exposed.

White found nothing better than **2 ♗a1** and then came **2 ... ♖df8! 3 ♖xf3 gxf3!**.

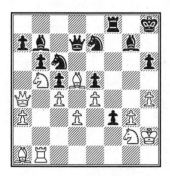

White to play

Suddenly h3 goes from being one of the least significant squares on the board, like a1 or b8, to the most important. White has no satisfactory way of meeting ... ♗c8 followed by the devastating ... ♕h3+.

He tried **4 ♘e3** but his kingside collapsed after **4 ... ♗c8! 5 g4 h5!** and he resigned in five moves.

Targets = Initiative

Chess can be a simple game if we forget about positional subtleties and just look for targets. A few pages ago we saw how a plan was just a matter of figuring out how White could get his pieces to attack g7. In the same way, an initiative can be nothing more than a series of threats to different targets. For example:

Moiseenko – Dvoirys
Feugen 2006

White to play

What matters most here? The players disagree: Black would like to think it's his extra pawn. White prefers to believe it's his lead in development.

But development comes with an expiration date. If White doesn't convert it to another asset, Black will catch up. Then the extra pawn will count more.

White played **1 ♕a3!**. The first point is that e7 is a target that loses the game after 1 ... 0-0? 2 ♗xe7.

The second point is White has a threat, 2 ♘b6!, since 2 ... ♕xb6? 3 ♕xe7 is mate and 2 ... axb6 drops the Exchange, 3 ♕xa8.

The tactics become easier to spot when you realize that the rook at a8 as well as the king are vulnerable. For example, after 1 ... f6 White plays 2 ♖ab1! and Black meets the ♘b6 threat with 2 ... ♘d7.

White to play

Now 3 ♗g4 is strong in view of ♗xd7+!. White can punish 3 ... f5 with 4 ♘d6+! exd6 5 ♗xd8 or 4 ... ♔f8 5 ♕b3! and ♕f7 mate.

Let's stop for a moment and consider an alternative to 1 ... f6. As ugly as it looks, the backward step 1 ... ♗f8 defends e7. It stops the 2 ♘b6 threat without incurring a weakness the way 1 ... f6 does.

After **1 ... ♗f8** White can renew the ♘b6 idea with 2 ♖ab1. He can then meet 2 ... b5 with 3 ♘a5 with considerable pressure.

But in the game White had a different idea, exploiting a newly vulnerable Black piece.

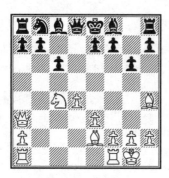

White to play

Which piece? Well, just look for one that became unprotected as a result of 1 ... ♗f8.

That's right, it's the rook at h8. Once you see that, it becomes easier to spot ways to attack it, with **2 d5!**.

This is based on 2 ... ♕xd5 3 ♘b6, again winning the Exchange. But it's also based on **2 ... cxd5 3 ♕c3!**, which threatens both 4 ♕xh8 and 4 ♘d6+! ♕xd6 5 ♕xc8+.

For example, 3 ... d4 4 exd4 ♗g7 invites 5 ♘d6+! ♕xd6 6 ♕xc8+ ♕d8 7 ♗b5+ ♘d7 8 ♗xd7+ or 7 ... ♘c6 8 ♕xb7, winning in either case.

In the game, Black played **3 ... f6**. But **4 ♘d6+!** works one more time, e.g. 4 ... exd6 5 ♗xf6 or 4 ... ♕xd6 5 ♕xc8+ ♔f7 6 ♗b5! (better than the immediate 6 ♕xb7 ♕c6).

Targets in Defense

Both attacks and initiatives are fueled by targets. But for the defender, a target means something else: It's a source of counterplay. A target is the difference between active and passive resistance.

That's the choice Black faces in the next example and, as often happens, passive defense is losing defense.

Abreu – Nataf

Havana 2001

Black to play

White has a basic winning plan of bringing his king to the queenside, say to c3, and pushing the b-pawn. A king and passed pawn generally can outmuscle a lone rook. It's as simple as two against one.

A master would see that Black can stop that plan with 1 ... ♖e7. But he would also realize that cutting off the king that way allows White to win with 2 ♔f2 and 3 b4!, followed by 4 ♖b2, 5 b5 and so on.

Black's only chance of survival is to create a kingside target for his king. If he can pick off a pawn there and create his own passed pawn, Black may draw.

A typical way to start is 1 ... ♖b4 and 2 ... f4. But White can anticipate that with 2 f4!.

For example, after 2 ... h5 3 ♔f2 ♔g6 4 ♔e3 h4! White could just keep going to the queenside, 5 ♔d3! hxg3 6 hxg3.

Black is slow in exploiting the target, and 6 ... ♖b3+ 7 ♔c4 ♖xg3 8 b4 turns out to be a win for White. No better is 6 ... ♔h5 7 ♔c3 ♖b8 8 b4 ♔g4 9 ♖d3!.

So let's go back to the diagram and see if we can speed up Black's counterplay. The right way is **1 ... f4!** and then **2 gxf4 ♔f6** and ... ♔f5.

Both of Black's pieces were active after **3 ♔f2 ♔f5 4 ♔g3 ♖b6!**. Black's rook is perfectly placed. It can check at g6 or b3, depending on circumstances.

This was evident after **5 ♖c2 ♖g6+ 6 ♔f2 ♖b6!**.

White to play

There is no win in 7 ♔e3 ♖b3+!. Or in 7 ♔g3 ♖g6+!.

34

White can only set a trap with **7 h3**. Then 7 ... ♔xf4? 8 ♖c4+! and 9 b4! allows him to bring his king to the queenside and win.

But Black avoided this by answering 7 h3! with **7 ... ♖b3!**. There were no other tricks and a draw was reached soon after **8 ♔g3 ♖b6 9 h4 h5 10 ♖c8 ♖g6+ 11 ♔f2 ♖b6**.

How do you acquire the habits of a master? Some master traits may be unattainable. Many masters simply concentrate better than non-masters. Bobby Fischer was not the only GM who boasted of how "beautiful" he thought.

But most good habits of masters can be learned. For example, you can train yourself to 'always look for targets' by clicking through games slowly and making a note, mental or written, every time a newly visible target appears.

Positional, rather than tactical, games are more suitable for this. And master games tend to be better study material because too often in amateur games, play becomes chaotic and there are simply too many targets. When you click through a game, or play it over on a board, look at it from White's point of view. When you're done, replay it from Black's perspective. Regardless of who won, you should be able to make target searching part of your chess routine.

Lazy Pieces

Looking for targets is the most important of the good habits of masters. The second most important is:

A master makes his pieces work harder.

Books and teachers are always telling novices: Put your pieces on good squares and good things will happen to them. Even in a position that seems quite equal, getting a bishop, knight or rook to the right square can make a big difference.

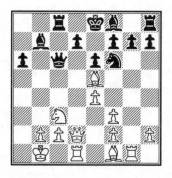

Goloshchapov – Mishra
Dhaka 2002

White to play

There is one White piece that has yet to be developed: the bishop at f1. Ideally, what's the best square for that bishop?

Masters think like that. When you open up your mind that way you find master-moves like **1 ♗c4!**.

The bishop is going to b3, a perfect square. It will not only protect the king position by blocking the b-file but will also create a powerful threat of ♗a4 and ♗xf6/♗xd7+. In fact, after 1 ... d6 the retreat 2 ♗b3! followed by ♗a4 would win the game.

Of course, to play 1 ♗c4 White had to have an answer to **1 ... ♛xc4**. But it wasn't hard to find one, **2 ♗xf6**, which threatens 3 ♛xd7 mate.

The best Black could do after 2 ♗xf6 was to protect d7, with 2 ... ♗c6 or 2 ... ♛c6. But he is lost after 3 ♗xg7 ♗xg7 4 ♖xg7.

Masters get more out of their pieces. It's not because they have more pieces. Or smarter pieces. They have the same pieces you have.

But they get theirs to work harder. A master isn't satisfied with a bishop that controls a nice diagonal or a rook that dominates an open file or a knight that occupies a central outpost. Their pieces have to *do something*, not just look good.

Abramovic – Savon
Erevan 1982

Black to play

If you were to ask yourself, "Which is Black's best-placed piece" you might answer "The bishop." It has a nice, clean diagonal. It denies White's heavy pieces the use of squares such as d2 and e3.

But that's not enough. If you look for targets, your eyes should focus on the other side of the board. What matters most to Black is the pawns at b2 and c2. They are targets and can come under fire after ... ♘a4.

However, Black can't carry out a queenside raid yet because 1 ... ♘a4 2 ♘xa4 ♛xa4 3 ♘b3 ♛xa2 allows White to take off a more valuable pawn, 4 ♖xd6 or 4 ♛g4 and 5 ♛xe6+..

That explains **1 ... ♗e7!**. The bishop looked nice on g5 but on e7 it does something: It protects the d-pawn and that means 2 ... ♘a4! is a powerful threat.

There followed **2 ♖d3 ♘a4! 3 ♘d1 ♛c7!**.

White to play

One of the threats, ... ♛xa5 or ... ♛xc2, must succeed. With his queenside in collapse, White threw himself into an attack, **4 ♛g4**, threatening ♛xe6+. But he eventually lost after **4 ... ♖f6 5 ♖g3 ♗f8 6 ♘b3 ♛xc2**.

Moving the Furniture

Because there are so few unoccupied and safe squares in a typical middlegame, it stands to reason that the right square for one piece may be unavailable because it belongs to another. To make his pieces work harder, a master rearranges them. He 'moves the furniture around', often with surprisingly strong effect.

Stahlberg – Keres
Munich 1936

Black to play

Each of Black's pieces appears well-placed. His knight is splendidly centralized and his bishop controls several key squares. His queen rook commands the open file.

But Black realized that his pieces don't have targets. If his rook penetrated on the file, 1 ... ♖c2?, it walks into 2 g4!. His pieces look nice – but they're lazy.

37

That explains **1 ... ♘f6!** followed by ... ♗e4-d5. Then White pawns come under fire on both wings, at a2 and g2 and he can drive the White knight off e5 with ... d6.

Things didn't appear to change much after **2 ♖ac1 ♗e4!** until White began to search for a reply to 3 ... ♗d5!.

If he protects the a-pawn with 3 a3, then 3 ... ♗d5 4 ♕a4?! d6 5 ♘c6? ♕d7 loses material. And 5 ♘c4 allows 5 ... ♗xf3 6 gxf3 ♘d5 and ... ♘f4, when the underused KR joins the action.

There are other problems with 4 ♕d3?! d6 5 ♘c4 because of the pinning 5 ... ♕c7!.

That's why White went in for the complications of **3 ♘g5 ♗d5 4 ♕h3**.

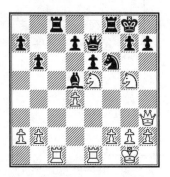

Black to play

White is relying on tactics, such as 4 ... ♗xa2 5 ♖a1 and ♖xa7, or 4 ... ♕b4? 5 ♘xd7! ♘xd7? 6 ♕xh7 mate.

But **4 ... ♖xc1 5 ♖xc1 h6!** kicked one of knights back so that Black can get the upper hand after 6 ♘gf3 ♕b4 7 b3 d6 8 ♘c4 ♘e4.

Instead, White gambled on **6 ♘g6 ♕e8 7 ♘xf8 hxg5 8 ♖c7 ♕xf8 9 ♖xa7.** Material is roughly equal.

But as often happens when the queens remain on the board, a rook is no match for two minor pieces because the queen works more efficiently with a knight or bishop than with a rook.

Black to play

Black was winning after **9 ... ♕b8! 10 ♖a3 ♕f4 11 ♕e3 ♕f5 12 ♖c3 ♕b1+**

13 ♖c1 ♛xb2 14 ♛xg5 ♛xa2. But the real winning moves were 1 ... ♘f6 and ... ♝e4-d5.

Work it or Trade it

When you hear someone say that master chess is 'more concrete', what they mean is that variations trump appearances. Another illustration of that: If a piece – even a good-looking one – isn't pulling its weight, a master looks for a way to get rid of it.

Karpov – Macieja
Warsaw 2003

White to play

This had been a fairly even game until five moves before, when White forced Black to give up his dark-squared bishop for a knight. White's bishop on c5 should give him a serious positional advantage.

But there's a limit to what the bishop can do. White realized that the easiest way to make further progress was **1 ♝xb6!.**

A knight will do more on c5 than a bishop because it attacks a6 and b7 (**1 ... ♘xb6 2 ♘c5**).

Then White prepares to invade on the dark squares, not with the departed bishop, but with the queen on d4 or d6 (e.g. 2 ... e5 3 ♛d2 and 4 ♛d6).

The game went **2 ... ♛a8 3 ♛e5 ♝c6**.

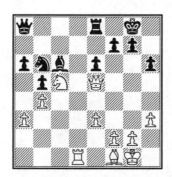

White to play

Black seems to have everything covered – until White makes a full-board search for targets. Then he notices g7 and finds **4 ♖d4!.**

Black doesn't have a good defense against 5 ♖g4, which threatens ♕xg7 mate and that prompts another weakness, such as 4 ... f6 which can be punished by ♕g3 followed by ♖d6 or by ♗d3/♕g6.

In the end Black desperately sought a trade of queens and lost the endgame after **4 ... ♕b8 5 ♕xb8 ♖xb8 6 ♘xa6**.

Often, two good habits fit together to produce a good move or plan. Don't be frightened by the word 'plan'. A plan is usually just two or three useful moves that fit together. Here's an example.

Glek – Krivoshey
Bundesliga 2004

White to play

White has the usual kingside pressure that he enjoys in this kind of pawn structure. His bishop and knight cooperate nicely against the target at f7.

But there's no way to aim another piece at f7. That suggests that either White's bishop or knight isn't doing enough. For that reason he switched to **1 ♘g4!**.

He threatens 2 ♘h6+ ♔h8? 3 ♘xf7+ and would be happy to see 2 ... ♗xh6 3 ♗xh6 (or 3 ♕xh6) and 4 ♖e3.

White would also like to meet 1 ... ♘d5, which closes the b3-f7 diagonal, with 2 ♗h6 and see if his majority of pieces on the kingside can overwhelm the Black king.

But there's a more important explanation for 1 ♘g4 and it was revealed by **1 ... ♘xg4 2 ♕xg4**.

Black to play

The elimination of Black's knight means that two targets have been exposed, at h7 and e7. White can aim at them with ♕h4 and/or ♖e3-h3.

In addition, f7 is still vulnerable if Black uses his KR to defend e7 – 2 ... ♖e8? 3 ♕f4! forces 3 ... ♖f8 after which 4 ♖e3 and ♖ce1 is unpleasant.

Black does have a target of his own, c3, to shoot at and he can shoot with **2 ... ♕c8!**. White was only slightly better after **3 ♕g3 e6 4 h4!** and then **4 ... ♗d5! 5 ♗xd5 exd5 6 h5**.

One of the best ways to train yourself to get more out of your pieces is – once again – to reexamine your losses. When you lose a game positionally, or even when you got mated, there was probably a piece (or pieces) that you mishandled. After you resigned you may have concluded that you lost because of, say, an opening mistake or getting a bad pawn structure. But there was almost certainly a lazy piece that cost you. Take another look at those games.

If you'd prefer study material that is less of a threat to your ego, play over games of Bobby Fischer, Anatoly Karpov, Magnus Carlsen, Michael Adams or one of the other grandmasters who rarely seem to have bad pieces – and managed to skillfully dispense with them if they did.

Low-Calc Thinking

Masters are more efficient with their pieces – and with their calculations. They trained themselves to be that way. A third good habit to acquire:

A master doesn't calculate more than he has to.

Let's be honest. The best players can calculate very, very long variations. They can see much farther ahead than you. But masters are also more practical. They know that the longer the variation a person tries to calculate, the more likely he will miss something. The likelihood escalates if he's tired from calculating other long variations earlier in the game.

Shirov – Carlsen
Moscow 2007

White to play

Black's pieces appear so much more vulnerable that White would be justified in trying to find a forced win. Candidate moves such as 1 ♖d7+, 1 ♘d5 and 1 ♘g4 might occur to you.

White focused on another idea, winning the unprotected bishop. He looked at 1 g3 with the idea of 1 ... ♗g5 2 ♖d7+.

White wins the bishop after 2 ... ♔h6 3 ♕h1+!. Or after 2 ... ♖f7 3 ♖xf7+ ♔xf7 4 ♕d5+ and ♕xg5.

But there is a complication. Black can meet 1 g3 with 1 ... ♗xg3, based on 2 fxg3?? ♕xe3+.

Still, White didn't want to give up on a strong-looking move like 1 g3 and he worked out a win: 1 ... ♗xg3 2 ♖d7+ ♔h6 3 ♕h1+! ♔g5 4 ♖d5+ ♔f4 and now 5 ♕h3!.

All very neat. But in the end White chose **1 ♕e4!** instead.

Black to play

He had the same goal, winning the bishop. But this is much simpler, and the chance of making a mistake in calculation is much less.

This time the bishop has no good move at all (1 ... ♗g5 2 ♕e7+ ♖f7 3 ♕xg5 or 2 ... ♔h6 3 ♘g4+).

Protecting the bishop also fails: 1 ... g5 2 ♕e7+ ♖f7 allows 3 ♘f5+ followed by a winning rook check at d6 or d8.

Black couldn't find a defense and resigned after **1 ... b3 2 axb3**.

Even though he didn't find a flaw in his calculation of 1 g3, White went with the safer and simpler queen move – because it is safer and simpler.

Masters recognize that they can often get a better read on a position by evaluating it in general terms, rather than calculating.

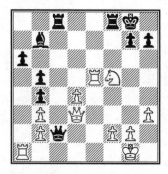

Karjakin – Onischuk
Khanty-Mansiysk 2010

White to play

Black has just captured on c2, offering to trade queens. There is a lot for White to calculate, beginning with 1 ♕xc2 ♖xc2 2 ♘d6 and 1 ♖d1 ♕xd3 2 ♖xd3.

He can also stay in the middlegame with 1 ♘e7+ followed by a queen move such as 2 ♕g3. Even a GM could easily spend half an hour trying to work out all the lines.

But, White wrote, "Here it isn't necessary to see all the variations. It's sufficient to evaluate the position." He went on: "White dominates the center and kingside, and Black's bishop doesn't help in the defense."

He concluded that he should go after the king with **1 ♘e7+ ♚h8 2 ♕g3** and rely on solid moves to provide him with threats.

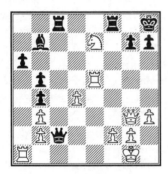

Black to play

One of the low-calculation techniques is visualizing. This means looking in general terms at the near future: What good moves are available to you? What are the best squares for your pieces?

At the previous diagram White might have concluded 1 ♘e7+ and 2 ♕g3 was best because he could see ♖ae1-e3 coming up, as well as ♕h4, with prospects of ♘g6+. This went into White's favorable evaluation of this position.

Calculating is different from visualizing because you have to take your opponent's moves into consideration. But you can reduce the amount of calculation by just getting a taste of a few sample variations.

For example, White might have looked at 2 ... ♕xb2 because it looks the most dangerous. The natural response is 3 ♖ae1. White can see a variation that runs 3 ... ♖c1 4 ♘f5 g6 5 ♘d6. Of course, this is only one variation. But if he likes the looks of it, White can feel confident enough to go ahead.

Sample variations are not expected to be conclusive and often they don't occur in the game. In fact, Black chose **2 ... ♖cd8** rather than 2 ... ♕xb2. Then came **3 ♖ae1 ♕d2 4 ♖1e3 ♕xb2** but White's attack was overwhelming after **5 ♕h4**, e.g. **5 ... ♖d6 6 ♖f5! ♖a8 6 ♕f4 ♖dd8 7 ♖f7 resigns**.

Visualizing plays an important role in determining whether you have winning chances in a particular line of play you're considering. We'll explore that further in Chapter Six. But here's a taste:

Lautier – Cvitan
Ohrid 2001

White to play

White had this kind of position in mind when he made decisions several moves ago. But why did he think he could win this? After all, the pawns lie on only one wing. Black has doubled pawns but they do a good job of preventing White from creating a passed pawn.

Actually this is a simple win if you visualize what it would be like if a pair of rooks has been traded. Suppose the rooks on c4 and f8 disappear.

In positions like that, Jose Capablanca would say, "White wins in one move." He was joking: the one move is White king to e8.

In other words, once a pair of rooks is gone, what White needs to win is to attack the only available target, at f7. Black could either lose the f-pawn or advance it, creating a new target at g6. Then it's just a matter of applying pressure to whatever is weakest.

Play continued **1 Rdc7! Kg7 2 Rc8! Rxc8 3 Rxc8**.

Black to play

Thanks to his ability to visualize, Capa-like, a winning future position, White didn't have to calculate what follows. The game went **3 ... Bd4 4 Rc4 Be5 5 Rc6 Kf8 6 Kf1 Ke7 7 Ke2 Kf8 8 Rc5 Bf6 9 Rc7 Be5 10 Rb7**.

White could have chosen other squares for the rook without damaging his winning chances. The next stage was to advance the king towards e8. Play went **10 ... Kg7 11 Kd3 Bd6 12 Kd4 Bf4 13 Kd5 Kf6 14 g3! Bd2 15 Kd6 Be1 16 Rb1 Bc3** (not 16 ... Bxf2 17 Rf1).

44

Once the king is closing in on f7, White frees his rook from the defense of his pawns by advancing them to light squares – **17 ♖b3 ♗e5+ 18 ♔d7 ♔g7 19 ♖b7 ♔f8 20 g4 ♗d4 21 f3 ♗e5 22 ♖b5 ♗f4 23 ♖c5 ♗d2 24 ♖c8+! ♔g7 25 ♔e8**.

Black to play

There is no defense to White getting his rook to the seventh rank. On 25 ... f6, the easiest way to win is to get White's king to e6 and sacrifice the rook on f6 for a bishop and a pawn.

In the game Black tried **25 ... f5 26 ♖c7+ ♔f6** and White went after the new target at g6 with **26 ♔f8!**, threatening ♖c6+. He won shortly after **26 ... ♔e5 27 ♔f7 ♔f4 28 ♔xg6**.

Must-Calc

There are, naturally, bound to be times in a game, particularly a complex game, when you absolutely must calculate. High on the list are situations when you are defending.

Defense tends to require more exact and thorough calculation than attack. On the other hand, when you have the initiative or are simply better developed, you can sometimes rely on a calculating minimum.

Kholmov – Suetin
Leningrad 1963

White to play

White's advantage in development is minimized by the well-placed Black queen and knight. To White, those pieces are what matters most.

There is a way to deal with them, **1 ♕e3!?**. But to play this White has to calculate 1 ... ♕xe3 2 fxe3.

White realized it was worth calculating. He saw 2 ... ♘g6 3 ♘b3 would give him a sizable edge after 4 ♘c5 or 4 ♖d6 (or after 3 ... ♗a6 4 ♗xa6 ♖xa6 6 ♖d7).

But he knew he wasn't done. He also had to calculate 2 ... ♘e6 and he saw that this time his knight should go to f3 because e5 is a target. After 3 ♘f3 ♗a6 4 ♗xa6 ♖xa6 5 ♘xe5 White has a big edge (5 ... ♘c5 6 ♘d7!).

Finally if Black meets 1 ♕e3! with 1 ... ♘e6 he is losing a pawn to 2 ♗xe6 ♕xe3 3 ♗xf7+.

That's a lot to see. But it was worth it because to avoid all this Black had to retreat his queen. It was a big concession, as the game went: **1 ... ♕e7 2 ♘b3 ♗e6** and now **3 ♗xe6 ♘xe6**.

White to play

White has a positional advantage because of the queenside targets (a5 and c6). He could restart his calculating machine and consider lines such as 4 ♕b6 ♕g5 and then 5 ♕xc6 ♘f4 (threat of mate on g2) 6 g3 ♕g4 or 6 ... ♖ac8.

But it's just not worth it. White's advantage has become more obvious since the previous diagram and he deserves an easier time.

He can increase his positional edge – without calculation – by just doubling rooks on the d-file, ♖d2 and ♖fd1. Play went **4 ♖d2! c5 5 ♖d5 c4 6 ♘c5 ♖fc8 7 ♘xe6 ♕xe6 8 ♖fd1**.

Then came **8 ... ♕c6 9 ♖b5 c3 10 b3! ♖d8**.

White to play

Amateurs sometimes reach commanding positions like the one White enjoys. But they become frustrated because they haven't been able to cash in yet. They try to calculate forcing lines like 11 ♖xd8+ ♖xd8 12 h3, which threatens ♖xe5 or ♖xa5.

They may see that 12 ... ♕c7 13 ♕c5 looks good for White. But they aren't sure about 12 ... h6 13 ♖xa5 ♖d2! and try to look further and further ahead. And meanwhile their clock is running.

A master knows that keeping command of the position – **11 ♖bd5! ♖xd5 12 ♖xd5** – is what matters most. Then he can take his time probing both wings.

Play went **12 ... ♕f6 13 g3 h6 14 ♕d3 ♔h7 15 h4 ♕e6 16 ♔g2 f6 17 ♖d6 ♕f7 18 ♕f3**.

On the kingside he was looking at 19 h5 followed by ♕f5+ and possibly ♕g6 or ♖d7. Black defended with **18 ... h5 19 ♕d3 ♖a7 20 ♖d8 ♕g6 21 ♕d5 ♕f7**.

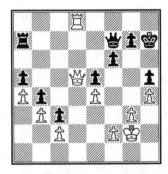

White to play

For the first time in 20 moves White should calculate a long variation. Why now? Because **22 ♕xf7 ♖xf7** and 23 ♖a8 ♖d7 24 ♖xa5 ♖d2 or 23 ♖d5 ♖a7 changes the position decisively, one way or the other.

In fact, White is winning in the **23 ♖d5 ♖a7** line if he finds **24 f4! exf4 25 ♖xh5+ ♔g6 26 g4!**. It takes a further examination – of **26 ... ♖d7 27 ♖d5! ♖xd5 28 exd5** – to prove it.

But the position in the diagram was the last one before the time control. White didn't have time to calculate 22 ♕xf7!. He kept control of the situation with 22 ♕d3 and eventually found a way to win, 16 moves later.

Reducing calculation to a minimum is a more difficult habit to acquire than the others discussed in this chapter. One training method might help:

After each of your tournament games, try to remember the variations that you calculated. You don't have to recall every single move. Rather, you should try to recollect the candidate moves you spent significant time on and whether you looked three, four, five or more moves into the future. (You might be able to make this part of a post-mortem analysis with your opponent, or even record it.)

Some time later, go over the game again and see how many variations that you looked at were wastes of time and energy. You'll probably find that the best moves you played could have been selected with a fraction of the time you spent on them. This can show you how much more efficiently you can think.

And now for this chapter's quiz positions.

Quiz

7

Vallejo Pons – Shirov
Ayamonte 2002

Black to play

Black can't be too confident about his material edge in light of his mangled pawns. What is his best policy?

8

Chandler – McNab
British Championship 1988

White to play

How can White prove he has more than equality?

9

Volkov – Vaganian
Moscow 2005

White to play

How many potential targets can you identify for White? What should he do?

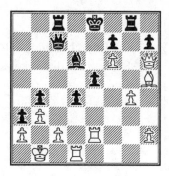

10
Leko – Rodriguez
Yopal 1997

White to play

White is poised to win on the kingside. How does he nail down victory?

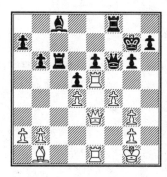

11
Morozevich – Petrushin
Krasnodar 1997

White to play

White's positional advantage is clear in view of his better bishop and more concentrated rooks. How can he make progress?

12
Short – Svidler
Moscow 2002

Black to play

That great knight on c4 and passed b-pawn give Black an edge. How does he win?

13
Mikhalchishin – Jelen
Slovenian Championship
2002

White to play

Is this the time for White to calculate or maneuver? And if so, calculate what and maneuver how?

14
Tukmakov – Lazarev
Neuchatel 2002

White to play

Should White begin calculating variations directed at the kingside? He can defend b3 with 1 ♗d1, for example, and then play 2 ♕d2/3 ♗h6+ or 3 f4.

15
Smyslov – Spassky
Moscow-vs.-Leningrad 1959

White to play

Should White be thinking of targets or about getting more out of a lazy piece?

Chapter Three:
Little Tactics

You know what tactics are. They are the decisive moves you use to decide the majority of your games. Most of the other moves on your scoresheet may seem like filler, passes that you made until you can pin a queen, skewer a rook or fork two pieces.

But a master uses tactics in a different way. Sure, many of his games end the same ways that yours do, when his opponent cannot meet tactical threats. But to get to that point a master builds up a position, usually slowly, until it is overwhelming.

To do that he uses two types of move that most amateurs rarely employ. One type is forcing and positional. That is, the move gets its energy from tactics. Typically it's a simple threat to win something. But its primary purpose is to obtain better chances in a positional way, such as by improving the placement of a bishop or knight or weakening enemy pawns or forcing the trade of a strong enemy piece.

These are 'little tactics'. They make seemingly minor, almost trivial changes in the position, in contrast to 'big tactics', the ones that win games. Here is an example of little tactics in action.

McShane – Carlsen
London 2010

White to play

White has more pieces developed but as usual that's only a temporary advantage. Most of his edge may disappear after ... ♘c5.

In most cases, a lead in development can only be exploited by tactics. In this case, that suggests **1 ♘c6**. The main points of it are:

(a) White threatens to win with 2 ♘xe7+ and 3 ♘xd6, and

(b) After 1 ... bxc6 2 bxc6 he threatens 3 ♖xb6, and

(c) He also sets up a elementary pitfall, 2 ... ♕xc6?? 3 ♘f6+, which costs the queen.

There were other tactical elements to 1 ♘c6. For instance, if Black replies **1 ... bxc6 2 bxc6** and then **2 ... ♛c7**, White would regain his sacrificed material with **3 cxd7**. Then **3 ... ♗xd7** leads to this.

White to play

White still has a lead in development and again he can exploit it tactically, with **4 c5!**. His threat to win a pawn, 5 cxd6, would prompt 4 ... dxc5. Then another tactic, 5 ♖b7 ♛xb7 6 ♘f6+ and ♗xb7, favors White nicely.

But if that was all there was to 1 ♘c6 – a one-move threat to win the e-pawn, a cheap trap for Black to fall into and a few other tricks – there wouldn't be much to White's knight move. Black would simply defend his pawn, as he did in the game, with **1 ... ♖e8**.

That's how many amateurs play chess. They make tactical moves in the hope that their opponent will overlook their point. When their opponent doesn't miss the threat, their move turns out to be just a waste of time.

But there was more to 1 ♘c6!. Its main purpose was purely positional. White's knight looked good on d4 but it wasn't doing enough. He wants to plant it on a much better square, d5. He got closer to that with **2 ♘b4!**.

Black to play

If White can play 3 ♘d5 it's not just a one-move threat. It squeezes Black's position, e.g. 3 ♘d5 ♛d8 (or 3 ... ♛a5) 4 b6 threatens 5 ♘c7.

Black understood the danger and reacted sharply, with **2 ... f5 3 ♘c3 ♛c5**. This is the practical approach to defense: When your position is in decline, rely on tactics. Black pinned the b4-knight and prepared an attack on the c-pawn

(... ♘e5xc4). In addition, he set a pitfall, since 4 ♘xa4 can be met by the pinning – and apparently winning – 4 ... ♛a7.

But White was able to fight tactics with tactics. After 3 ... ♛c5?, he fell into the trap, **4 ♘xa4! ♛a7** because he had seen **5 ♘a6!**.

Black to play

This meets the 5 ... ♛xa4 threat and prepares to win with 6 ♘c7.

Black had nothing better than **5 ... bxa6** after which **6 b6** is far superior to 6 ♗xa8.

Black managed to avoid dropping material after **6 ... ♘xb6 7 ♖xb6.** But he had steadily lost ground in the positional battle that began with 1 ♘c6!. White piled on more forcing moves, **7 ... ♖b8 8 c5! ♗e6 9 ♖db1 dxc5 10 ♖b7,** and **Black resigned** soon after **10 ... ♖xb7 11 ♖xb7 ♛a8 12 ♘xc5**.

Separate Boxes

Most players regard moves as being either tactical or positional. They like to divide and distinguish them, putting them in separate boxes. That makes studying easier. They can look at White-to-play-and-win positions to sharpen their tactical skill. They can look at a master game with positional themes to understand what strategy is all about.

But this blinds them to the benefits of a forcing positional move, like White's play in the next example.

Hertneck – Vaganian
Bundesliga 1992

White to play

White's basic idea is to attack and win the d5-pawn, say with ♘de2-f4 and ♕d2/♖fd1.

But Black has several defenses including ... ♘e4 and ... ♘e6, depending on circumstances. Quiet White moves, which is another way of saying non-forcing moves, may not overcome those defenses.

White's solution was **1 b4!**, forcing Black to choose a square for the knight immediately. Then 1 ... ♘e6 rules out ... ♘e4 and allows a strong 2 ♘de2!.

So Black replied **1 ... ♘e4.** But White followed up with two more forcing moves. He played **2 ♘xe4**, intending to answer 2 ... dxe4 with 3 ♘c6!.

The attack on the Black queen gives him either a favorable endgame (3 ... ♕xd1 4 ♖fxd1 and ♖d7 or ♗xe4) or a nice middlegame (3 ... ♗xc6 4 ♖xc6 or 3 ... ♕e8 4 ♕d6!).

But Black can use little tactics, too. He thought he had found a flaw in White's calculations so he met 2 ♘xe4 with **2 ... ♗xd4**, a zwischenzug (in-between move).

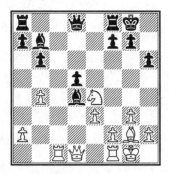

White to play

Black's point is that without a White knight – and with a Black pawn on e4, rather than d5 – there is no significant edge (3 ♕xd4 dxe4 or 3 exd4 dxe4).

However, the little tactics aren't over. White found a counter-zwischenzug. **3 ♘d6!**. Then Black has a glum choice between defending an isolated pawn middlegame (3 ... ♕xd6 4 ♕xd4) or going into the complications of 3 ... ♗a6.

The complications turn out to be awful – 3 ... ♗a6 4 ♕xd4 ♗xf1 5 ♗xd5! and now 5 ... ♕xd6? 6 ♗xf7+ costs the queen while 5 ... ♗h3 6 ♗xa8 ♕xa8 7 e4 leaves Black a pawn down with little compensation.

Black chose **3 ... ♕xd6** and was condemned to defense after **4 ♕xd4 ♖ad8 5 ♖fd1 f5**, otherwise 6 e4!. He eventually lost after **6 ♕b2 ♖f7 7 ♖d4 ♕e5 8 ♖cd1** and ♕d2.

Petite Combinaison

Tactics are not the same as combinational play. A tactical move typically makes a threat. A combination typically offers a sacrifice. Both may secure a positional advantage. Jose Capablanca was famous for making a *petite combinaison*, a little combination. Here's a modern example of a little combination followed by little tactics.

Grischuk – Giri
Monaco 2011

Black to play

Black played **1 ... c5**. There is sound reasoning behind this: After 2 dxc6 bxc6 the improved piece play Black receives on the b-file may matter more than the targets he creates at a6 and c6.

But 1 ... c5? is an oversight. He was surprised by **2 ♘e6!**, which exploits the presence of Black's king at the end of the b3-g8 diagonal.

It doesn't appear that the king matters in a position like this because there are pawns at d5 and f7, blocking the diagonal. Yet the combination works because after **2 ... fxe6 3 dxe6** White has three threats. One is the obvious 4 exd7+.

Black to play

But the others are 4 ♗xd6! and 4 ♖xd6!, based on 4 ... exd6 5 e7+, which would win the queen.

Black made the best of a bad deal by getting his king off the diagonal, **4 ... ♔h8**.

After **5 exd7 ♕xd7** the combination is over and we can appreciate the fruits it bore White. He enjoys several positional plusses, including the two bishops, the isolated e7-pawn and the exploitable hole at e6.

There are a number of promising moves to consider, including 6 ♗f3 and 6 ♘a4. But White played **6 ♕b6!**, threatening both 7 ♕xc5 and 7 ♗xd6 exd6 8 ♖xd6.

Black to play

Black again tried for b-file play with **6 ... ♛c6.** But after **7 ♕xc6 bxc6 8 b3!** he had amassed *four* weak pawns.

Add to that the slimness of Black counterplay, and it amounts to a positionally lost game. He **resigned** after trying another trick, **8 ... ♞fe4 9 ♞xe4 ♝xe5**, which allowed **10 ♞xc5 ♜a8 11 ♞d7!**.

Looking back, we can detect a difference. The little combination, 2 ♞e6!, gained several advantages. The little tactic, 6 ♕b6!, was less forcing. But its threat to win a pawn secured a won endgame.

Boris Gulko, the only player to win the championships of the Soviet Union and the United States, grew up as a fan of Mikhail Tal. What he particularly admired in Tal's combinations is that when one was over, what was left on the board was not an 'and wins' position but one that had gotten somewhat better.

"They improve an equal position or turn a worse position into equality or, often, make an unclear position more unclear," Gulko wrote. In fact, in the game Tal called his favorite, the featured combination was essentially no more than a clever way of trading queens.

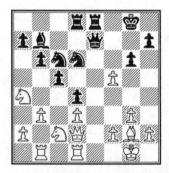

Smyslov – Tal
USSR Team Cup 1964

Black to play

White has just captured a pawn on f5. The routine 1 ... ♞xf5 promises little after 2 ♜e1.

Black tried **1 ... ♞e5!**, to trade bishops (2 fxg6? ♝xg2 3 ♚xg2 ♕b7+).

But White had a forcing reply, **2 f4**. He is not trying to win a piece with 2 ... ♗xg2 3 fxe5? because 3 ... ♗a8! and 4 ... ♕b7 would create devastating mating threats on the long diagronal.

Instead, he would meet 2 ... ♗xg2 simply with 3 ♕xg2!, pocketing a safe pawn.

Therefore Black answered 2 f4 with **2 ... ♘f3+ 3 ♗xf3 ♗xf3** and White came back with the obvious **4 ♖e1**.

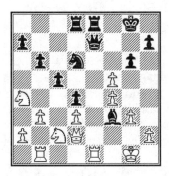

Black to play

Tal had foreseen this and replied **4 ... ♕e2!!** and **5 ♖xe2 ♖xe2**.

What most fans enjoyed was the might-have-beens: the winning variations that could have come about after 6 ♕c1 ♖g2+ 7 ♔f1 ♖xh2. Some lines run at least six moves more and include ... ♖e8-e2 and ... ♘f5xg3(+).

But many fans failed to appreciate that when White played the best move, **6 ♕xe2!** and then **6 ... ♗xe2 7 ♘b2! gxf5**, Black had reached an endgame that was only slightly better for him. It was enough to work with and Tal won 45 moves later.

Of course, you don't have to be capable of 12-plus-move combinations to become a master. But a much smaller *petite combinaison* is a master's stock in trade.

One Move Further

There's a second kind of little tactics. This one is also positional in purpose but it's non-forcing. A move of this kind doesn't threaten anything. But it needs a tactical justification to make it playable.

It comes about most commonly when a master sees a candidate move he'd like to play. Often it's a move he'd *love* to play. It improves his position considerably. But it seems to fail for a simple reason, such as putting a pawn or piece en prise.

The remedy is to look one move further. You try to find a tactical shot that makes the positional candidate playable.

Hellers – Petursson
Malmo 1993

White to play

White has more space and more targets. Black can't castle kingside because it would lose his h-pawn and likely his king as well.

But Black can put up a fight by maneuvering his knight to e4. He's not ready to do that immediately because ... ♘c5 would allow ♘xf5!, followed by ♗xc5 or ♘xg7+. However, Black can prepare with ... b6 and then ... ♘c5-e4.

With that in mind, White turned a merely advantageous position into a nearly winning one with **1 c5!**.

What's protecting the pawn? Tactics: 1 ... ♕xc5 is crushed by 2 ♘xe6.

Black is on slightly firmer ground if he takes with his knight, 1 ... ♘xc5. But then 2 ♖ac1 threatens 3 ♖xc5 ♕xc5 4 ♘xe6. If Black replies 2 ... b6, White ensures an edge with 3 ♘b3.

Some amateurs might consider 1 c5 because they see how taking the pawn brings swift punishment. But White didn't expect to win that way. He expected to just keep improving his position, as in the game, which went **1 ... ♘f8 2 ♖ab1!**.

Black to play

The c-pawn still isn't hanging (2 ... ♕xc5? 3 ♘xe6). But what makes 2 ♖ab1! a good move is that it sets up b7 up as a target.

He would win, for instance, after 2 ... ♘g6 3 ♖b6 ♘e7 4 ♖fb1 ♖b8 5 ♕f3 in view of 5 ... h4 6 ♖xb7, 5 ... ♘c6? 6 ♘xc6 or 5 ... ♘d5 6 ♘xf5!.

In the game, Black opted for **2 ... f6?**, which allowed a strong **3 ♕f3 ♖b8 4 ♖b6!**. The game ended with **4 ... fxe5 5 ♘xe6 ♘xe6 6 ♖xe6+ ♔f8 7 fxe5 ♔g8 6 ♕d5! resigns**.

Baby Steps

Little tactics can be difficult to appreciate because the changes they bring about are so slight, such as repositioning a lazy piece or opening a diagonal. Unless you can be sure that the repositioned piece is on a better square or the diagonal will matter, the change may have no benefit, or even backfire.

Let's see how a world champion used little tactics.

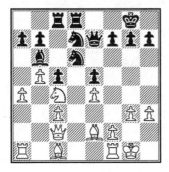

Botvinnik – Szilagyi
Amsterdam 1966

White to play

The first moves that catch the eye of most players are the forcing 1 a5 and 1 ♖d1.

Many players would prefer 1 ♖d1 for two reasons. It develops a piece, and the natural defense, 1 ... ♘xc4, allows White to post his light-squared bishop on a terrific diagonal, 2 ♗xc4.

But a master would want more out of the position, as we'll see in the next chapter. White's chances are already so good that he should check out another develop-with-tempo move, **1 ♗g5.**

It is tactically justified by 1 ... ♕xg5 2 ♘xd6. Moreover, White can see that if Black tries to avoid this by means of 1 ... ♘f6? he gets into a nasty pin. White can exploit it with 2 ♘e3! and 3 ♘d5.

So far, so good. But there are still at least two major questions. The first is: How good is **1 ... ♕xg5 2 ♘xd6** ? Has White improved his chances since the position in the previous diagram?

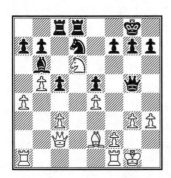

Black to play

He has. His knight is well placed at d6, and if the attacked Black rook goes to c7, the Black bishop is trapped by 3 a5!.

Moreover, if the rook goes to b8, White can take aim at another target, f7, in coordination with 3 ♗c4!. Then if Black defends with 3 ... ♖f8, White can choose between going after the b-pawn with 4 ♗d5 or increasing pressure with 4 ♖fd1.

That's a lot to calculate, and some players – even masters – would stop after they saw 3 ♗c4. Some – including masters – might stop after visualizing 2 ♘xd6 and conclude that the position just has to be good for White.

But two good outcomes – after 1 ... ♕xg5 and 1 ... ♘f6 – are not enough to justify **1 ♗g5**. The other big question White has to answer is whether he benefits after **1 ... f6**, since he has no better reply than a retreat, **2 ♗e3**.

That is what happened in the game, which continued **2 ... ♘xc4 3 ♗xc4+ ♔h8**.

White to play

White hasn't won material or created a vulnerable pin. But he improved his position considerably. He not only got his bishop to the good diagonal but that diagonal was extended to Black's first rank.

White proceeded to squeeze Black's minor pieces with **4 a5 ♗c7 5 ♖fd1 ♘f8**. Then **6 ♕a2!** stopped Black's knight from coming into play via ... ♘e6. White can visualize a mating attack by lining up his queen in front of the light-squared bishop and threatening ♕g8.

With so little room to operate in, Black swapped rooks, **6 ... ♖xd1+ 7 ♖xd1 ♖d8 8 ♖xd8 ♗xd8**. But after **9 a6 b6**:

White to play

White's superiority has grown again, and this is where the more familiar role of tactics – the game-winning 'big tactics' – comes in.

A good idea is to get his queen to d5, where it threatens that mate on g8 as well as an attack on the queenside pawns, ♕a8 or ♕b7. But after 10 ♕d2, Black has an adequate defense in 10 ... ♕d7!.

A better method is **10 ♕e2!** with the idea of ♗b3 and ♕c4. Black can defend against the ♕g8 mate idea by moving his knight and playing ... ♕f8. But he would be lost on the queenside, **10 ... ♘e6 11 ♕g4!** (threatening ♕xe6) **♘c7 12 ♕c8** and **♕b7**.

The point to appreciate here is that the key to White's victory was 1 ♗g5! f6. That one-move tactical line created a concession that proved to be huge. Black did not have a major improvement after 2 ♗e3, and soon after that White had a positionally won game, thanks to additional forcing moves like 4 a5 and 9 a6.

The Tactical Habit

The biggest obstacle to learning how to use little tactics is the mindset that tells you that tactics are used to attack. One way to rid yourself of this notion is to examine master games that have nothing to do with attack.

You might choose games with quiet openings, such as the more positional lines of the Queen's Indian, French, and Nimzo-Indian Defenses. After each move, try to find a tactical point. Don't rely on annotations to point them out. Annotators, particularly elite GMs, regularly omit mention of key tactical points. They seem to think they're too obvious and unworthy of their comment.

Don't expect every move that's played to have a tactical subtext. But appreciate the way a master blends tactics and strategy together. Consider the next example.

Bareev – Yudasin
Groningen 1993

White to play

The position of Black's queen suggests it can be exploited. But by 'exploited', we don't mean White should be able to win the queen or even a pawn. Rather, he can try for some positional plus, like a superior pawn structure or more space.

For example, he can drive the queen off the diagonal with 1 ♘e1 and then 1 ... ♕c8 2 ♗xb7 ♕xb7. Then he can try to seize control of the center with 3 e4.

But Black can use little tactics of his own, with 3 ... ♗b4!, intending ... ♗xc3/... ♕xe4. White's position deserves more than 4 ♘b5 a6 5 ♘d6 ♕c6 (6 ♖d1 ♘e8).

White's solution was the immediate **1 e4**. Black can't take the pawn because 1 ... ♘xe4 2 ♘e5! costs a piece.

That's a fairly primitive tactic. But it pays off in the positional column. After 1 e4! White has the better center and threatens to gain more space by pushing to e5.

If Black tries to discourage that with 1 ... d6, his bishop has no retreat from c5. It might be trapped if White can engineer b2-b4.

So Black played **1 ... ♗e7**, safeguarding the bishop and threatening 2 ... ♕xc4.

But White used his fine tactical sense to enlarge his edge with **2 e5! ♘h5 3 ♗e3!**.

Black to play

Again Black gets punished if he grabs a pawn, 3 ... ♕xc4? by 4 ♘d2 ♕c7 5 ♗xb7 and 6 g4, trapping the knight. (He might also be winning with 4 ♘g5, which threatens mate on h7 as well as ♗xb7.)

To safeguard his knight, Black played **3 ... f5.** But White wasn't done with little tactics. He shot back **4 ♘e1! ♕c8 5 f4!**, which gives him a big edge in space and a pawn structure that greatly favors his pieces.

Once again tactics stopped Black from grabbing a pawn, **5 ... ♗xg2 6 ♕xg2 ♕xc4?? 7 ♕xa8**.

Play continued **6 ... ♘a6 7 ♕e2!** – attacking the knight and prompting a new weakness – **7 ... g6 8 ♖d1 ♖d8 9 ♘f3 ♘c7 10 ♖d3 ♘e8 11 ♖fd1!**

Black to play

Rather than spend a tempo on 11 b3 to protect the pawn, White had figured out that 11 ♖fd1! ♕xc4 12 ♖xd7 leads to a big endgame edge for him.

Black managed to liquidate his worst weakness with **11 ... d6**. But thanks to White's little tactics – 1 e4! and 2 e5!/3 ♗e3! and 7 ♕e2! and 11 ♖fd1! – he had a substantial edge and eventually converted it to victory after **12 b3 dxe5 13 ♖xd8 ♗xd8 14 ♘xe5 ♗f6 15 ♕f3 ♖b8 15 ♘b5**.

Count it up and you'll find more than half a dozen threats and minor tactics. Looking at games like this should deepen your appreciation of little tactics. Among contemporary players, Vishy Anand, Vladimir Kramnik, Hikaru Nakamura and Magnus Carlsen regularly use little tactics to the full and their games are a rich source of study material. Among the older players whose games you might consider there is Samuel Reshevsky, Mikhail Botvinnik, Anatoly Karpov, Akiba Rubinstein, Svetozar Gligoric, Vasily Smyslov and Tigran Petrosian.

Yes, Petrosian. After one of Boris Spassky's world championship matches with Petrosian, he told Gligoric, "You know, Gliga, Tigran is first and foremost a stupendous tactician."

Happy Accident

Let's be honest. No one intentionally alternates tactical moves with strategic moves. No master says to says to himself, "I'm going to play something positional this turn and then next move it'll be time to find a pin or skewer that I can use." It just turns out that way, a happy accident.

Here's an example of mixing little tactics and positional moves from Yuri Averbakh, best known for his splendid endgame play and books.

Averbakh – Neikirch
Portorozh 1958

White to play

A few moves earlier White was pursuing a standard strategic goal in this opening, ♘e3-d5. If he had achieved it, Black would have been virtually forced – for tactical reasons – to capture the knight. White would then retake with his e-pawn, giving him a passed d-pawn, a wonderful outpost on e4 for his pieces and the c2-h7 diagonal for his light-squared bishop.

But Black discouraged that plan when he retreated his knight from c6 to e7 and puts his queen on c6. Now 1 ♘d5? just loses a pawn.

However, Black's regrouping has a drawback. White underlined it when he played **1 c4!**.

Normally, he would be reluctant to reinforce control of d5 this way because it creates a hole at d4 that Black could occupy with a knight. But after ... ♘e7/ ... ♛c6, it's gotten hard for Black to do that.

So far this is purely positional thinking: outposts, passed pawn, hole. Black replied **1 ... ♘e8**.

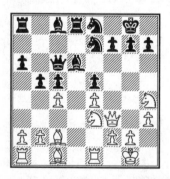

White to play

Black has a strategic goal of his own, occupying d4 by a different route, ... ♘c7-e6-d4!.

White cannot stop that through positional means. That's the job of tactics and White found **2 ♗b3!**. He threatens 3 cxb5! followed by ♛xf7+ and mates.

That exploits the knight's absence from f6. If the knight goes back, 2 ... ♘f6, White has another shot, 3 ♘g4!. That would lead to clear positional edge after

3 ... ♗xg4 4 hxg4 and 5 g5 or 3 ... ♘xg4 4 hxg4 with a renewed threat of 5 cxb5 and 6 ♕xf7+.

Therefore Black met the threat of 3 cxb5! with **2 ... b4**. However, this enabled White to resume improving his game positionally, with **3 ♘d5!**, the move he's wanted to play for several turns.

When Black replied **3 ... ♕b7**, White improved another of his pieces by means of **4 ♗a4!**.

Black tried to the same with **4 ... ♘c7**.

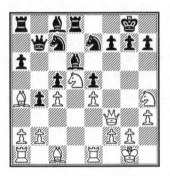

White to play

The Black knight is headed once again for d4 via e6. But White found another way to deter him and, naturally, it was tactical, **5 ♗g5!**.

He threatens to win a piece or more with 6 ♗xe7 ♗xe7 7 ♗c6! (7 ... ♕xc6?? 8 ♘xe7+ and ♘xc6).

And what about 5 ... f6 ? Well, there are few Black pieces defending his king so White believed 6 ♘xf6+ gxf6 7 ♗xf6 had to give him a winning attack.

Black had run out of ideas and he accepted the consequences of **5 ... ♘cxd5 6 cxd5 f6 7 ♗e3**.

Since his light-square bishop has no particularly good square he traded it off, **7 ... ♗d7 8 ♗xd7 ♕xd7**, and there followed **9 ♖ac1 ♖dc8 10 ♖c4! ♖ab8 11 b3 ♖c7 12 ♖ec1**.

Black to play

White has a positionally won game. He may not be able to crack through the queenside defense because Black has committed all his pieces there is. Instead, White switched to the kingside and eventually won after **12 ... 罝b5 13 g4! g5 14 ⊘g2 ⊗g7 15 h4**.

Tactical Technique

Most players have an uneasy feeling about composed studies. They don't like those 'White to play-and-win' positions they see in magazines because they seem artificial.

Yes, most studies are very artificial. But what amateurs might like about them is that the solutions are usually 100 percent tactical. You don't have to know esoteric, technical positions. Just work out the tactics.

In fact, one of the best ways to improve your winning technique is to work on endgame tactics. Technique is mainly a mixture of little tactics combined with progress-making moves, such as creating a passed pawn. Here's a dramatic but not unusual example.

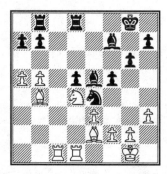

Taimanov – Spassov

Slanchev Breag 1974

White to play

White had employed few tactics to build up his positional edge. But to convert that edge he needed threats, and he began with **1 a6!**. This is based on the elementary 1 ... bxa6? 2 ⊘c6 fork.

Black made another concession with **1 ... ⊗xd4 2 罝xd4** and should have continued 2 ... bxa6 4 bxa6 罝dc8, now that the fork was eliminated. His position had declined thanks to 1 a6 but is not yet lost.

However, he tried to used his own tactics with the immediate **2 ... 罝dc8** and **3 罝xc8+ 罝xc8**.

His point is that 4 axb7? 罝b8 and 5 ... 罝xb7 not only regains his pawn but makes the White b5-pawn as much of a target as his own a7-pawn.

White to play

But White had another trick, **4 b6!**, to get a protected passed pawn to the seventh rank (4 ... bxa6 5 b7 ♖b8 6 ♗xa6). That would win swiftly.

Black chose **4 ... axb6** instead but after **5 axb7 ♖b8 6 ♗a6** he was lost.

He might have tried one last trick with 6 ... ♗e8 so that he rids himself of the dreaded pawn after 7 ♖xd5 ♗c6 and ... ♗xb7.

But this fails – tactically, of course – to 7 f3! and then 7 ... ♘f6 8 ♗d6 or 7 ... ♘c5 8 ♗xc5 bxc5 9 ♖xd5 because of the 9 ... ♗c6 10 ♖xc5 ♗xb7 11 ♖b5! pin.

Black to play

Instead, Black played **6 ... ♗e6** and resigned after **7 ♖xe4!** – in view of 8 ♗d6.

By playing over endgames like that, or entire games by Magnus Carlsen, Vladimir Kramnik, Anatoly Karpov or any of the other great players mentioned earlier in this chapter, you should enjoy a greater appreciation of how to become what *every* master is: a positional tactician.

And now for some quiz positions:

Quiz

16
Anand – Topalov
Monte Carlo 2000

White to play

What is White's biggest problem and what should he do about it?

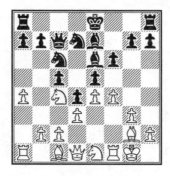

17
Piket – Timman
Amsterdam 1996

White to play

White's position looks nice but what specifically can he do?

18
Botvinnik – Tal
World Championship 1961

White to play

How does White improve his position?

19
Vaganian – Huebner
Thessaloniki 1984

White to play

How does White establish a positional advantage?

Chapter Four:
More

At a memorial service after Bobby Fischer's death in 2008, the Philippines master Renato Naranja recalled how they both competed in the 1970 Interzonal tournament. One day, after Naranja had drawn with a Soviet grandmaster who was much stronger than him, Fischer told the Filipino he stood better when the game ended.

Yes, I know, replied Naranja, but I couldn't see how to win. Fischer said that was no reason to agree to a draw. When you *know* you have an edge, you just keep playing, he said. "You had the two bishops," Fischer said. "Just move around."

This is another major difference between masters and amateurs. Masters want *more* out of a position. They try to win – and find ways to win – positions that seem unlikely to be winnable. Here's a vintage example.

Kmoch – Gruenfeld
Vienna 1922

Black to play

Black played **1 ... f5.** This was "a big surprise" for Larry Evans when he annotated the game. He gave the move a '?!' to label it as dubious. "This move would never occur to me," Evans wrote.

There are several reasons why it wouldn't. It's not a developing move. It restricts Black's QB. Moreover, Black has good alternatives, such as 1 ... ♖e8 or shifting his bishop to e6 and d5. These alternatives are so firmly based on general principles that – barring a tactical problem – they have to be good.

But Evans was 16 when he wrote, "This move would never occur to me." Already a master, he knew a lot about playing. But he had a lot to learn about winning.

What he didn't appreciate is how drawish the position becomes if Black plays purely according to principle. After 1 ... ♖e8, White can play, say, 2 c3 ♗d6 3 d4. There is little to prevent him from playing other principled moves, such as ♗e3, ♕d2, ♖fe1 and ♗f4 or ♗g5. Then the position is so evenly balanced, there is no friction. It will get closer and closer to a draw after each of the inevitable piece trades.

Black didn't want a draw. He was a stronger player than White and he followed Siegbert Tarrasch's advice. A master offers "silent odds" whenever he plays a weaker player, Tarrasch said, so he has to find ways to avoid a draw.

This doesn't mean taking risks. In this game Ernst Gruenfeld wasn't making bad moves in the hopes of confusing White.

No, he was simply giving White more chances to go wrong after 1 ... f5. (There were very few ways to go wrong after 1 ... ♖e8.) And Black had a logical way to do that:

The first step is ... ♗d6 followed by ... ♕h4, threatening mate on h2.

Then, if White defends with g2-g3, Black's queen will retreat to f6 and he will try to open the kingside with ... f4!. On the other hand, if White defends with h2-h3 he is vulnerable to ... g5-g4.

Evans wrote that the strange 1 ... f5 inexplicably worked "like a charm" as the game continued **2 d3 ♗d6 3 ♗d2 ♕h4 4 g3 ♕f6 5 ♗c3 ♕h6**.

White to play

If White meets ... f4 with g3-g4, Black can continue ... ♕h4 followed by ... g5 and ... h5! with a fierce, if not winning, attack.

White preferred **6 ♖e1 f4 7 ♗g4**. But this allowed **7 ... fxg3 8 fxg3 ♖f2!**. As stunning as that may appear, it is a known sacrificial device.

In this case, **9 ♔xf2 ♕xh2+ 10 ♔e3 ♕xg3+ 11 ♕f3 ♗g4 12 ♕xg3 ♗xg3** would land White in a bad endgame (or in the losing 11 ♗xf3 ♗g4! and ...♖e8+.).

Instead, he inserted **9 ♖e8+ ♗f8** and then **10 ♔xf2 ♕xh2+ 11 ♔f1**. But **11 ... ♗xg4! 12 ♕xg4 ♖xe8** eventually won for Black.

Afterwards it was pointed out that 10 ♗h5! would have held for White. But that doesn't detract from 1 ... f5!. It gave White ways to go wrong. Instead of being able to rely on routine moves in a sterile position, he was soon fighting for a draw.

Prolong!

Masters want more. And because of that, they often get it. It sounds too simple but it's true.

There are specific ways to emulate masters in this way. But ultimately it comes down to Fischer's attitude: If you keep pressure on your opponent long enough, if you keep forcing him to make choices – if you keep trying to win – there's a good chance that you will.

This view was also a tenet of the Soviet School. Mikhail Botvinnik's watchword was "Prolong! Prolong the struggle." Think twice about trading pieces when you have the advantage, he said. Continue the pressure, even if you have to temporarily retreat.

Salov – Anand
Wijk aan Zee 1998

Black to play

Black had made considerable progress in the previous five moves. He advanced his bishop from f6 to b2, where it pressures the a3-pawn and watches for the chance for a tactical shot on c1. He moved his rook up from c4 to c2, where it pins the knight. And he shifted his queen from c8 to h5, from where he can invade at h2, giving check.

It looks like Black can deliver a knockout with 1 ... ♖c1. For example, 2 ♘xc1 ♕xd1 wins the queen and 2 ♕d7 ♕h2+ 3 ♔f3 allows mate after 3...♕h1+.

But White can refute 1 ... ♖c1 with 2 ♕xc1! ♗xc1 3 ♘xc1. His king cannot be separated from the rook and knight (3 ... ♕h2+ 4 ♔e1 ♕g1+ 5 ♔d2 and 6 ♘e2!). They in turn defend the only targets, the pawns at g3 and a3. This is what is called a 'fortress.' Black cannot win.

But the position in the diagram isn't even and is hardly drawish. Black may retreat his attacked rook. But that just means moving the furniture. Or in Fischer's terms, 'just moving around'.

Black played **1 ... ♕h2+ 2 ♔f3 ♖c8!**.

White to play

Black doesn't have a specific threat. But he can visualize, again without calculating, that the rook would be effective if it reaches h1 or h2.

He can also see how hard it is for White to find safe moves. For example, if his queen leaves the first rank, such as 3 ♕d3, he allows a strong 3 ... ♕h1+! so that 4 ♔g4 ♕h5 mate or 4 ♔f2 ♖h8!, threatening 5 ... ♖h2 mate.

A computer might find a defense, perhaps with a rook move. But a human in White's chair would be reluctant to risk putting his rook on an unprotected square such as with 3 ♖e7.

In the end, White played **3 ♕b1.** Black found a way of making progress, **3 ... ♗c1! 4 ♘xc1 ♕h1+** and **5 ... ♖xc1.**

For example, 5 ♔e2 ♖xc1 6 ♕b3. Now if Black looks for ways to 'just move around', he would find 6 ... ♕g2+ 7 ♔d3 ♖c6!, with a killing threat of ... ♖d6+/ ... ♕d2 mate.

Instead, White played **5 ♔f2 ♖xc1.**

White to play

To stop the threat of ... ♕f1 mate, White played **6 ♕d3.** But **6 ... ♖g1!** prompted **resignation** (7 ♕e4 ♕h2+ 8 ♔f3 ♖f1+ or 7 ♕c3+ ♔h7 8 ♔e2 ♕g2+ 9 ♔d3 ♖d1+).

Good, Better, Best

Show two experienced players a complex position, and they are both likely to find a good move. The stronger player is likely to find it faster. But he's also more likely to keep looking once he's found it.

As good as the move may appear, the master looks for a better one. That often makes the difference of a half-point, if not a full one.

**Sasikiran –
Kasimdzhanov**
Hyderabad 2002

Black to play

Black is a pawn ahead but there are a lot of tactics that skew attempts to evaluate the position.

The first point to notice is that White's last move, 1 ♖c1, appears to win material in view of 1 ... ♕d8 2 ♖c8 or 1 ... ♕b8 2 ♘d7.

The second point is that Black can avoid that fate with 1 ... ♘h3+ followed by winning the White queen with ... ♖xf1+.

When some amateurs make a discovery like that, they're strongly tempted to bang down the knight with check, with hardly any thought. But 1 ... ♘h3+ would turn out badly. After 2 gxh3 ♖xf1+ 3 ♕xf1 ♖xf1+ 4 ♔xf1 Black cannot save his queen (4 ... ♕d8 5 ♖c8).

A more experienced played would look further. He might notice that the ... ♘h3+ idea can be reworked by playing 1 ... ♕b8. Then he can meet 2 ♘d7 with a much better version of the check, 2 ... ♘h3+ 3 gxh3 ♖xf1+ 4 ♕xf1 ♖xf1+.

Of course, that's better than 1 ... ♘h3+??. But a master wants even more.

Because the position is pretty tactical, he would sense there's an even better use of the ... ♘h3+ idea. Black came up with the stunning **1 ... ♗g5!!**.

White to play

When Black first noticed this possibility he probably calculated 2 ♖xc7 ♘h3+ and concluded that 3 gxh3 ♗xe3+ 4 ♔g2 ♖xf1 leaves a complex position.

If you look further, you'll see 2 ... ♘e2+! is much better than 2 ... ♘h3+?. White is lost, 3 ♕xe2 ♗xe3+ 4 ♕xe3 ♖xf1+ or 4 ♔h1 ♖xf1+.

White was strong enough to see the same variations after 1 ... ♗g5 that Black did. White didn't take the queen but played **2 ♕d2!**, which takes most of the punch out of ... ♗xe3+.

True, Black can still use the ... ♘h3+ idea in yet another form. He can answer 2 ♕d2! with 2 ... ♕xb6 3 ♗xb6 ♘h3+ 4 gxh3 ♗xd2. Black would have the edge in the endgame after, say, 5 ♖xf7 ♖xf7 6 ♗c2.

But Black still wanted more. He played **2 ... ♕e7!** because he has much better chances than White if queens remain on the board. Play continued **3 ♖fe1 ♕f6**.

White to play

Black can improve his position with ... ♕g6 and ... h4 and followed by ... g3 or ... h3 or even ... ♘h3+, depending on White's play. White's pieces are protected and coordinated but they can't do much.

And when White did try to do something, **4 ♖c8?**, he lost immediately to – guess what? – another knight check. After **4 ... ♘e2+!** **White resigned** in view of 5 ♕xe2 ♗xe3+ 6 ♕xe3 ♕f1+! and mate or 6 ♔h1 ♗xb6, with an extra piece for Black.

The clear superiority of 1 ... ♗g5!! over the other candidate moves was revealed by calculation. More often the difference between alternatives is much less. What makes one candidate good, another better and a third best may simply be a matter of how many chances each one gives your opponent to go wrong.

Bjornsson – Tal
Reykjavik 1964

Black to play

White threatens to win the Exchange with ♗xf8. Black can foil that with the simple 1 ... ♕xd2+ and then 2 ♖xd2 ♖fd8. He would have slightly the better of, say 3 ♗e3 ♘f4. But winning would require some bad White moves.

A more enterprising idea is 1 ... ♗g5. This time White will have a bad bishop, such as after 2 ♗xg5 ♕xg5 or 2 ♕xd8 ♖fxd8 3 ♗xg5 ♘xg5.

This may be more winnable for Black – or rather more losable for White. If White later allows a trade of his knight for Black's bishop he will likely lose. The same goes for allowing Black's king to invade along the dark squares, ... ♔h6-g5-f4.

But Black looked for more. He realized that he might be able to allow ♗xf8. He could dominate the dark squares with ... ♕xf8, ... ♗g5 and ... ♕h6, followed by ... ♘d4 or ... ♘f4.

If Black is willing to offer the Exchange, the best way would seem to be a queen move, to avoid 2 ♕xd8. But 1 ... ♕e7 2 ♗xf8 ♕xf8 3 ♕d7! is problemsome.

Black looked for something better and found it in the remarkable **1 ... ♗c6!**, one of the last moves you might consider. It eliminates the annoying ♕d7 and prepares ... ♕e7.

White can trade queens after 1 ... ♗c6 but he is worse after 2 ♕xd8 ♖fxd8 3 ♖xd8+ ♖xd8 4 ♗e2 f5 or 4 ... ♘f4. Also poor for him is 2 ♕d6 ♕xd6 3 ♖xd6 ♖fc8 and 4 ... ♘d4.

That left **2 ♗xf8 ♕xf8**:

White to play

Now 3 ♕d6 fails because Black can regain the Exchange favorably with 3 ... ♕xd6 4 ♖xd6 ♘d4 and ... ♗e7.

But the main benefits of 1 ... ♗c6! became evident when White made the mistake of staying in a material-up middlegame, with **3 ♗d3?**. Black's control of the dark squares gave him a solid edge after **3 ... ♗g5** and **4 ♕f2 ♕h6**.

For example, 5 ♘e2 ♗e3 6 ♕g3 ♘f4 7 ♘c3 ♘h5! 8 ♕g4 ♗d4! and the Black queen invades at e3.

In the game, White tried **5 ♘f1** and was losing soon after **5 ... ♖d8 6 g3 ♘d4** and **7 ... f5**. But the main reason he lost is that 1 ... ♗c6! gave him more ways to lose.

Move Loyalty

There's another way that a master's desire for more works for him: He doesn't give up easily on a move he really wants to play. He remains loyal.

We saw how this works with a positional candidate in the last chapter. If a master really likes the positional features of a move he will try to find a tactical justification. The same goes for a tactical candidate move.

Vorobyev – Belov
Moscow 1998

White to play

Black has just played ... ♗b4. It looks strong because ... ♗xc3 as well as ... ♘a4 are threatened.

But White noticed that the bishop is also unprotected. The first idea that comes to mind is 1 ♘xd5 so that 1 ... ♗xd2 2 ♘xc7+ or 1 ... exd5 2 ♕xb4. But on closer inspection, this fails to 1 ... ♘xd5!, protecting the bishop.

That's enough reason to give up on 1 ♘xd5 – but not to give up on the idea of exploiting that bishop. White saw that **1 ♘cxb5** has the same 2 ♘xc7+ and 2 ♕xb4 ideas as 1 ♘xd5.

However, once again there's a problem. Black can meet 1 ♘cxb5 with the countershot **1 ... ♕c5**. He defends his bishop and leaves White's knights vulnerable.

White would lose material after 2 ♘c3 ♕xd4 or 2 c3 axb5 3 cxb4 ♕xd4.

White to play

White saw all this when he played 1 ♘cxb5 but he didn't reject the move. Instead he searched for a counter to the counter-shot. He found **2 ♘b3!**.

Black's queen is also attacked and a retreat, 2 ... ♕f8?! makes 3 c3! strong this time.

The only hard calculation required of White once he spotted 2 ♘b3 is to check out **2 ... ♗xd2 3 ♘xc5**. He concluded that 3 ... ♗xe1 4 ♘d6+ and 5 ♘xc8, or 3 ... ♘xc5 4 ♘d6+ ♔d7 5 ♘xc8 ♗xe1 6 ♘xb6+ must be good for him. He was right and won.

The American grandmaster Walter Browne was renowned for his move loyalty. In a U.S. Championship tournament, he emerged from a standard opening variation, on the White side of a Petroff Defense. The position after 13 moves had been played many times before, but never by Browne.

He spotted a bizarre, tactical move, putting a bishop on h6, where it threatened ♗xg7 but also allowed ... gxh6. The more he looked at it, the more he couldn't find a reason why it failed. Common sense told Browne that a strange move like 14 ♗h6!?! couldn't refute such a solid opening. But Browne refused to abandon it. He calculated and calculated and eventually played the move – and won.

Loyalty to an attractive candidate is another good habit. But to stick with a move, it must pass a cost-benefit test. It's worth spending a significant amount of time trying to justify the move you want to play if it would make a significant change in your winning chances. If it doesn't make a big difference, it's not worth the lost minutes.

Karjakin – Gelfand
World Cup 2009

White to play

Black had just traded off his QN on d4. He wants to develop his QR more aggressively than normal, via a6. He expected 1 ♘d2 ♖a6! 2 ♘f3 ♖g6, with a threat of ... ♗xh3 and good chances.

But White crossed him up with **1 ♖e1**. Black could see that it threatened 2 ♗xd5 ♕xd5 3 ♖xe7.

If Black has to defend against the threat with 1 ... ♗e6 or 1 ... ♗f6, he shelves his kingside plans for the QR. His prospects would shift from ambitious to modest.

Nevertheless, Black really liked the rook lift. "Having seen this move I understood that it had to be played!" he wrote. And that meant he looked at **1 ... ♖a6 2 ♗xd5 ♕xd5 3 ♖xe7 ♖g6**. To him, it was a must-calculate situation.

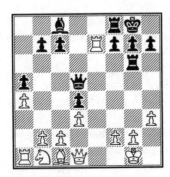

White to play

Black threatens mate on g2. He saw that 4 g3 ♗xh3 would give him good chances and he liked 4 g4 f5 so much that he was willing to try 1 ... ♖a6. (In fact, 4 g4 can be answered strongly with 4 ... ♕h5! followed by ... ♕xh3, ... ♗xg4 or ... f5.)

In the end, White declined the sacrifice. Thanks to his refusal to abandon 1 ... ♖a6! Black got the edge after 2 ♕h5 ♘b4 and eventually won. (Even better was 2 ... ♗b4! 3 ♗d2 ♘f4! 4 ♕f3 ♖f6.)

"My Turn"

Psychologists have found, through experiment after experiment, that people have stronger feelings about losing than about winning. Economists, who also analyzed this phenomenon, gave it a name, 'loss aversion'. And experienced chess players know it as the curious feeling that the joy of winning a game never quite makes up for the pain of losing one.

This helps explain why many amateurs fight desperately – and skillfully – in a bad position. But then they relax when they realize the danger of losing is past.

An amateur who survives a strong attack as Black may say, "Good, now I can look forward to playing White in my next game."

A master in the same situation will say, "Good, now it's my turn to play for a win in *this* game."

Adams – Zhukova
Gibraltar 2010

Black to play

White had missed two winning lines in the time scramble as well as a third that would have brought Black to the verge of defeat. Now that the time control was reached, Black could catch a breath.

She saw that the worst was over because 1 ... ♖b1 (or 1 ... ♖a1 and 1 ... ♖c1) followed by 2 ... ♛d1 should draw. Then her threat of mate on g1 (or h1 if White's queen leaves the diagonal) would force White to draw by perpetual check.

Considering what had gone before – and how much stronger a player White was – Black might have been expected to play a rook move quickly. Instead, she spent half an hour in thought.

But she wasn't rechecking her analysis or looking for a simpler way to draw. No, she wanted to know if Black had any winning attempts.

Only after failing to find any did she go into the drawing sequence of **1 ... ♖b1! 2 ♕e4 ♛d1 3 ♕xe6+ ♚d8 4 ♕f6+ ♚c8 5 ♕xa6+ ♚b8 6 ♕b5+ ♚a7 7 ♕a4+ ♚b8 8 ♕b5+ ♚a7** and so on.

And let's go back to Fischer one more time. After 44 moves during an Olympiad team tournament in 1970, his opponent, a friend, said "I don't know who is better, Bobby, but I offer a draw."

Fischer was candid when he refused: "I don't know who is better either but I have an extra pawn." Only when both sides were reduced to pass moves, 16 moves later, did he accept the draw. That's the spirit of a master.

And now some quiz positions:

Quiz

20
Carlsen – Nepomniachtschi
Wijk aan Zee 2011

Black to play

Black has perpetual checks at f3 and g4. Should he try for more?

21
Smyslov – O'Kelly
Groningen 1946

White to play

Each of White's pieces seems better than its opposite number. What can he make of that?

22
Madl – Chiburdanidze
Batumi 2000

Black to play

White has two pawns in return for the Exchange and his last move, 1 ♗b6, wins material.

As Black you see that 1 ... ♕xc3 leads to mate after 2 bxc3 ♖d1+ 3 ♖xd1 ♖xd1+ 4 ♔b2 ♗c1+ and 5 ... ♗a3.

But White can ignore the queen sacrifice and reply to 1 ... ♕xc3 with 2 ♗xd8. What do you make of that?

23
Lputian – Ivanchuk
Montecatini Terme 2000

Black to play

Black has given up a pawn to force White's pieces to bad squares. The natural move is 1 ... ♗xd4.

How good is that? What other moves should you consider? And which is best?

24
Ivanchuk – Blatny
Sharjah 1985

Black to play

White has two extra pawns. What should Black be thinking?

25
Gurgenidze – Tal
Gori 1968

Black to play

Black can try to rid himself of his slightly bad bishop with 1 ... ♗e5 and then 2 ♖ab1 ♗d4. Is there anything better?

Chapter Five:
Sense

Many amateurs believe that becoming a master is all about what you know. Masters know more technical chess information, like extensive opening analysis, exact endgames, and the like.

That's an excuse. You can say, "If only I had the time to study and digest that mass of information, I'd make master, too. I'd know what a master knows." But a master also has an edge over you because of what he *senses*. That's much harder to acquire.

For example, a master has a better sense of danger. Giving a simultaneous exhibition he will quickly make luft in one game as he moves on to the next board. It's not because of what he knows or what he calculated. It's simply his sense that this was the right time to play h2-h3.

Here's a similar case.

Topalov – Gashimov
Linares 2010

White to play

If an amateur is presented with this position, he might search for a forced mate and start by looking at 1 ♕b8.

A master would certainly consider it. But once he saw that there's no quick win he'd be attracted to **1 ♔g2!**. When White annotated this game he explained that it was the kind of useful move that a master plays automatically.

How is it useful? It protects the h-pawn, the only potential target for Black. It also eliminates the only tactical dangers, such as a first-rank problem after ... ♖c1+ followed by ... ♕c4-f1(+).

A master also has a better sense of when his opponent is running out of good moves. Here Black's pieces are as well placed defensively as they are going to be. Therefore 1 ♔g2! may force him to weaken his defenses.

That succeeded because instead of a super-passive pass like 1 ... ♖b6, he chose **1 ... h6?**. That created a fatal target at h6, e.g. **2 ♕b8 ♕f6 3 ♖h8!** (3 ... ♔g6 4 ♕f8).

We call this a sense of danger but we could also call it a feeling or an awareness. You can't always be certain that playing a particular move is risky. But a master develops a feeling for which positions are too risky to be worth playing.

"You think 'Such and such a move can't be played, it is too scary for a human' ", is the way Garry Kasparov put it. "A human can't defend such a position in a real game!"

There are other senses that give a master an edge, even against computers. In an endgame, a machine has no way but calculation to determine whether it is close to imposing zugzwang. A master can sense when he's getting close to it.

But the most important master sense is of timing. A master not only has a better feel for what to do in a position but how urgently it must be done. This tells him what kinds of candidate moves he should be looking at: Sharp and tactical? Or slow and strategic?

It also tells him how much calculation he should be doing. Without that sense, a player may end up wasting time and energy, looking too long at too many moves that are wrong for the position.

Most of all this sense tells him *who time favors*. If you're an experienced player, you already have some sense of that. You know, for example, that urgency is demanded when you've made a sacrifice.

Anand – P. Nikolic
Groningen 1997

White to play

White has the better development but Black has an extra pawn. That alone suggests that time is on Black's side. If he's allowed to coordinate his forces, say with ... ♕c7, ... ♘e7-c6, ... ♘c5, ... ♗d7 and ... 0-0-0, he will have a big, perhaps decisive edge.

With that in mind, **1 c4!** and then **1 ... dxc4 2 ♗e4** was right. White gave up a second pawn to create threats (♗xb7), energize his pieces (♗b4-d6) and make it difficult for Black to castle into safety.

Black was able to stop ♗b4 with **2 ... c3**. But that was a stopgap measure because after **3 ♗e3** White was bound to regain one of the pawns and also open up the c-file for his rook, with ♗d4 and ♖e3xc3.

85

Play continued **3 ... ♕c4 4 ♗d4 ♘c5 5 ♖e3**.

Black to play

Thanks to 1 c4!, White has made almost all of the progress since the previous diagram. Understandably, Black decided to get rid of one of White's bishops, **5 ... ♘xe4 6 ♖xe4**.

Then he played **6 ... ♗d7**, to meet the threat of 7 ♗b6 ♕xe4 8 ♕d8 mate and to prepare 7 ... ♗c6 and ... 0-0-0. It doesn't take a master's sense to realize that White needs to keep making threats to prevent Black from consolidating. That led him to **7 ♖e3** and play proceeded with **7 ... ♘e7 8 ♖xc3** and **8 ... ♕d5 9 ♖c5! ♕e4 10 ♖c7**.

White is preparing ♗c5, uncovering an attack on the d7-bishop, and a possible Exchange sacrifice. He would win outright after 10 ... ♗c6 11 ♖xe7+ ♔xe7 12 ♗c5+ and ♕d6-e7 mate.

And he would be on the road to winning after 10 ... ♖d8 11 ♗c5!, e.g. 11 ... ♘d5 12 ♖cxb7 ♗c6 13 ♖b8!.

Instead, Black found **10 ... b5** and White replied **11 ♗c5**.

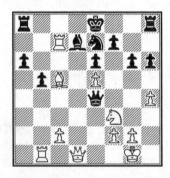

Black to play

Black can still defend, with 11 ... ♕d5 12 ♕e1 ♖c8! and the outcome would be unclear after 13 ♕a5.

But as often happens, the difficulty in meeting constant threats – "Prolong!" – got to Black. He blundered with **11 ... ♘d5? 12 ♖xd7! ♔xd7 13 ♖b4**, which costs the queen (13 ... ♕f5 14 g4).

This is the simplest kind of timing to appreciate. Time was Black's ally, and if White hadn't offered a second pawn (1 c4!) he would have lost in routine fashion. He likely would have lost if he had played quiet moves at any subsequent turn.

This is Morphy chess. But you need to know more than Morphy to make master.

Counterplay

Where a master's superior sense of timing stands out is when material is equal. Then an appreciation of other factors – particularly counterplay – tells him whether time is a factor and who it favors.

Malaniuk – Alexandrov, Minsk 1997: **1 d4 ♘f6 2 ♘f3 e6 3 e3 b6 4 ♗d3 ♗b7 5 0-0 ♗e7 6 c4 0-0 7 ♘c3 h6 8 e4 d5 9 cxd5 exd5 10 e5 ♘e4 11 ♕e2 ♘xc3 12 bxc3 ♕c8**

Malaniuk – Alexandrov
Minsk 1997

White to play

White has a choice of promising plans but kingside attack stands out. He controls more space there and there are potential targets at g7, h7 and h6.

But how should he attack? There are several ways:

(a) He could maneuver his knight with ♘e1-c2-e3-f5 and play for ♕g4xg7 mate.

(b) Or he could play 13 h3 and follow up with ♘h2 and then ♕h5/♘g4 followed by a piece sacrifice on h6.

(c) Or he could go line up his light-squared bishop and queen to threaten ♕h7 mate.

There are other options, as well. But instead of trying to calculate them, White needs to get a sense of the time frame. How long White can take for the attack will depend on how quickly Black generates counterplay.

Black doesn't have immediate threats and he is several moves away from making c3 a target. But he is ready to play 13 ... ♗a6!. A trade of bishops would neutralize White's best attacking piece.

True, White would still stand well. He can play on the queenside with 13 a4. If 13 ... ♗a6, then 14 a5, or 14 ♗xa6 ♕xa6 15 ♕xa6 ♘xa6 16 a5, with a slight edge.

But a master wants more. White concluded he had a legitimate chance for more but he didn't have the luxury of a slow buildup, with 13 h3 or 13 ♘e1. He chose **13 ♗b1!** instead.

Black set a trap with **13 ... ♗a6 14 ♕c2 g6**. This is based on meeting 15 ♗xh6? with 15 ... ♗xf1 16 ♗xf8 ♗xg2!, when suddenly he has counterchances.

But rather than try to figure out what happens then after 17 ♔xg2 ♕g4+, White chose the low-calc **15 ♖e1!**.

Black to play

Black is reduced to responding to specific threats, and play went **15 ... ♔g7** and then **16 ♕d2 ♖h8**.

Thanks to his inducing another kingside weakness (14 ... g6) White can just apply forcing or semi-forcing moves until Black's position disintegrates. There followed **17 e6!** and then **17 ... f5 18 g4!**.

Now 18 ... fxg4 would have lost to 19 ♕c2! ♕e8 20 ♘e5! followed by ♘f7 or ♘xg6.

Black tried **18 ... ♘c6** and there followed **19 gxf5 gxf5 20 ♕f4 ♕f8 21 ♕g3+ ♔h7 22 ♔h1!**. The game ended with **22 ... ♕f6 23 ♘h4 ♗d6 24 ♕h3 ♘e7 25 ♘xf5 ♔g8 25 ♘xd6 resigns**.

On the other hand, there are times when there is no urgency at all. A master knows when he can attack and take his time time doing it.

Hennings – McCurdy
Harrachov 1967

White to play

Unlike the last example, Black is developed and has a target, at c2 (1 ♖d2?? ♗g5). White's only advantage is space and the better bishop.

He played **1 c3** so that he could keep the queenside relatively closed (1 ... b4 2 c4). Play went **1 ... ♖5c7 2 h4 a5 3 ♔b1**.

But then came **3 ... a4?** and **4 a3!**. It may not be immediately obvious but White suddenly has a big advantage. Why? Because Black has no way to open the queenside short of (unsound) sacrifices on c3.

That means White has virtually unlimited time to carry out his own attack. He doesn't really have to calculate. When choosing a candidate he won't, in most cases, have to look more than a move or two into the future. He can follow a simple, general plan of safely advancing the g- and h-pawns.

Black tried to batten down the hatches with **4 ... ♗f8 5 g4 ♔h8 6 g5** and then **6 ... f6**.

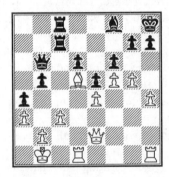

White to play

Black's pawn move changes the kingside options. It prevents f5-f6 and makes gxf6 possible.

But it does not change the timing. White can try one plan and, if it doesn't work, switch to another. He can 'just move around' without damaging his winning chances.

First he looked at doubling or tripling on the g-file. Play went **7 ♖hg1 ♗e7 8 ♖g3 ♖f8 9 ♖dg1 ♕b8**.

But it became apparent that ♕g2 followed by gxf6/ ... ♗xf6! will achieve nothing. Black will have ample protection of g7.

No problem. White simply shifted to another plan, eyeing the targets at d6 and b5. The game continued **10 ♕d2 ♗d8 11 ♔a1 ♕a7 12 ♗e6 ♕b6 13 ♖d1!**.

White is looking for a favorable opportunity to play gxf6 since now ... ♗xf6 hangs the d-pawn. He also eyes ♕e2 and ♖d5xb5.

Black seemed to have everything covered until **13 ... ♗e7 14 ♖d3 ♕c6 15 ♕e2 ♕b6?**.

White to play

White played **16 ♕h5!** so he can end the game with ♗f7 and then ♗g6. That idea had been in the air for some time but only works now that Black cannot defend in time with ... ♕e8.

The finish was cute. Black played **16 ... ♕b8 17 ♗f7! fxg5** with the idea of 18 hxg5 ♗xg5. But White replied **18 ♗g6! h6 19 hxg5 ♗xg5 20 ♕xg5! resigns**. Black would be mated after 20 ... hxg5 21 ♖h3+ ♔g8 22 ♖dh1 and ♖h8.

The difference between these two games is striking. In the first, Black's few developed pieces were not active. But there were things he could do (... ♗a6). White had to commit to attack (13 ♗b1!) or look for a more modest plan.

In the second example, Black's forces were well coordinated. But he had no targets after 4 a3!. White could take his time.

A good sense of time is intuitive. But it's a more difficult kind of intuition to acquire than, for example, realizing when a standard combination is available because you recognize a pattern. Critical moments don't fit a pattern.

Nevertheless, there are timing training methods. One that works particularly well with computers is to examine early middlegame positions from a database. You could go to one of the on-line databases, such as Chessgames.com, and look up at the games from a recent international tournament. Then, one game by one, click on each position after say, the 15th or 20th move.

Your aim is to see if you can evaluate urgency. Does time matter to one player more than the other? That is, will one side's position naturally improve over the next several moves if nothing dramatic happens? Does one side have to use its initiative, lead in development, whatever?

Once you've made an evaluation, see what did happen and whether one side or the other acted out of urgency. This will help deepen your sense of when you have to act.

Prophylaxis = Time Saved

Masters make all sorts of mysterious, aggressive moves in sharp positions. But some of the most mysterious don't seem to do anything. In a Sicilian Defense, when time seems to be a high priority, a master may spend a tempo to shift the White king from g1 to h1. Or, if castled queenside, from c1 to b1.

He does it to anticipate counterplay. Anticipating future threats is usually better than responding to immediate threats.

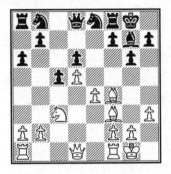

Smyslov – Filip
Vienna 1957

White to play

This is one of the games that made Vasily Smyslov famous. Great attention was paid to the stunning pawn sacrifices that ripped apart Black's kingside and the deft strokes that led to mate.

But that was much later. To enjoy the liberty of attack, White first had to secure the queenside, the home of most of Black's play. He began with **1 a4!** and **1 ... ♘d7 2 ♗e2!**, to discourage ... b5 as well as ... c4/ ... ♘c5.

Black persisted with the ... c4 idea and chose 2 ... **♕c7**. But White ruled that out with **3 ♖c1 ♖b8 4 b3!**.

So far White has pushed two pawns, retreated a bishop and placed his rook on a file that is unlikely to be opened. Yet he's made progress by denying Black his best chances for counterplay.

Black to play

Black wasn't done. He took aim at the e-pawn with his unused pieces, **4 ... ♘ef6 5 ♕c2 ♖fe8**.

After **6 ♗h2 h6** it was evident he had run out of counterplay ideas. But White still wasn't ready to go on the offensive with 7 f4.

He wanted to eliminate ... ♗d4+ and also to delay ... ♕a5. So he invested a tempo on **7 ♔h1!**, yet another prophylactic move.

Black, a world-class player, had his own sense of timing and realized that White is about to turn to a slow-building offense, with f2-f4, ♖ae1, ♗d3 or ♗f3 and e4-e5!. When only one side can make several moves of improvement – 'plus-moves' – the other side is almost always losing.

Black opted for **7 ... ♘h7**, threatening 8 ... ♗xc3 and 9 ... ♖xe4. He wanted White to play 8 f3, which interferes with his f2-f4 plan, or 8 ♗d3, which allows 8 ... ♘e5.

For the first time in the game, White had to calculate. He concluded that **8 f4!** was sound.

Black to play

He felt 8 ... ♗xc3 9 ♕xc3 ♖xe4 10 ♗d3 ♖e3 11 ♕d2 gives him plenty of compensation. Understanding 'comp' is another master trait and we'll explore it in Chapter Eight.

Black accepted the pawn in a different way, **8 ... f5 9 ♗f3! ♗xc3 10 ♕xc3 fxe4 11 ♗g4 ♘hf6 12 ♗e6+ ♔h7**.

A pawn storm is usually the slowest form of attack. But in the absence of counterplay, White felt it would succeed. It worked perfectly: **13 h4! ♖g8 14 g4! h5 15 g5 ♘g4 16 f5 ♖gf8 17 fxg6+ ♔xg6 18 ♗xg4 hxg4 19 h5+! ♔xh5 20 ♕g7!** and **White won** in a few moves.

Prophylactic moves, like 1 a4, 2 ♗e2, 3 ♖c1, 4 b3 and 7 ♔h1, sometime seem like a waste of time. But by killing counterplay they ultimately *gain* time for later. They gave White a free hand to finish the attack.

Note that 8 f4 was the turning point in the game. Recognizing those moments is another ability that marks a master.

Critical Positions

Reflecting on his long career, Boris Spassky said the greatest superiority he enjoyed over his rivals was a particular sense of timing: He had an uncanny feeling for when to mix it up, when to increase tension, when to force matters. "I was the king of critical positions," he said.

Hug – Spassky
Bath 1973

Black to play

Black seems to have an edge thanks to the knight at d4. White is reluctant to capture it because after ... cxd4, the c2-pawn becomes a target. But until White solves the knight problem, he can't move his queen to a good square and connect rooks.

Therefore, time should favor Black. He can make more useful moves – 'plus-moves' like ... ♖d7 or ... ♖ac8 – than White.

Nevertheless, Spassky felt this was the right time for **1 ... ♞xf3+! 2 ♗xf3**. The reason is that this gives him a chance to force a more favorable pawn structure with **2 ... c4!**.

The threat is 3 ... c3. A bit of calculation reveals that the defense 3 ♖e3 is as faulty as it looks. After 3 ... ♗c5 4 ♖e2 c3! 5 ♗xc3 White is in a mess following 5 ... ♗xf2+! 6 ♔xf2 ♕xc3.

So White replied **3 bxc4** and then **3 ... ♗b4! 4 c3 ♗e7**.

White to play

The point of Black's play was to create a glaring hole at d3 and a target at a4. He can exploit the hole with ... ♞d7-e5-d3 and the target with ... ♞d7-c5.

He can also exert pressure on the open file, e.g. 5 ♗a3 ♗xa3 6 ♖xa3 ♖d3 and ... ♖ad8. And if nothing else, he can regain a pawn favorably with ... ♞d7-e5xc4.

None of this would have been available if Black hadn't seized the moment with 1 ... ♘xf3+. Or, rather, if he hadn't sensed that this was a moment that could be a turning point.

It turned out to be the critical point of the game because White's position became progressively worse, **5 ♕e2 ♘d7 6 ♘b3 ♘e5**.

White saw that the c4-pawn was lost and tried to make the best of it with **7 c5 ♗xc5 8 ♘xc5?** – overlooking the crushing **8 ... ♖d2!** (9 ♕xd2 ♘xf3+). He would have been worse after 8 ♖ad1 ♘xf3+ 9 ♕xf3 ♗b6, intending ... ♕c4 or ... ♕c6.

Sensing when a position is critical frees a master to look for more candidate moves than he typically would. Normally, a master examines fewer candidates than non-masters. His intuition limits his search by pointing out the one or two moves that are likely to be best.

But his intuition is trumped by his sense that the position demands something more, a game-changing move, a *big* move.

J. Polgar – Kasparov
Prague 2002

Black to play

This position arose in a rapid match. The players didn't have time to calculate to their normal extent. But after White's last move, ♘c2-b4, Black could appreciate how precarious his situation was.

It wasn't the triple attack on the a-pawn that worried him. There's something that matters more, the d5 square. If White can plant the knight on that ideal outpost, Black's pieces, particularly his dark-squared bishop, will be stifled.

Black realized he needed a big move. That often means an 'impossible' move, one that you would normally dismiss without a glance. Here **1 ... d5!** was both impossible and very good.

Impossible because White controls d5 four times. Good because at the cost of a pawn Black obtains powerful tactical chances from ... ♗c5!.

White looked at 2 exd5 ♗c5 as well as 2 ♘xd5 ♗c5 and 2 ♕xd5 ♗e6. Each has its problems, so White went in for **2 ♗xd5** and then **2 ... ♗c5 3 ♗xa8**.

Black to play

Here Black had quite a bit to calculate because there was a real choice. Both 3 ... ♗h3 and 3 ... ♖g8 threaten mate on g2.

In the post-mortem, the players determined that 4 ♔f1 was the right answer to either move and would have favored White if Black had played 3 ... ♗h3? 4 ♔f1 ♗xf2 5 gxh3!.

Black chose **3 ... ♖g8! 4 ♔f1 ♗xf2** and eventually won. But if there was one thing that won the game it wasn't 3 ... ♖g8 or 2 ... ♗c5. Rather, it was the feeling that Black couldn't afford to play a routine move such as 1 ... a5, 1 ... ♗b7 or 1 ... ♗e6.

Not every game has a critical moment. Far from it. But there are enough examples in master chess to provide teaching moments. One way to benefit from them is to go through unannotated master games, either with a board or clicking through them on-line. Try to determine in each game whether there was a turning point.

What makes it particularly hard to sense turning points is that there are rarely road signs to identify them. A position may seem ripe for an irrevocable decision. But on closer inspection it might be better to delay it for a move or two.

Euwe – Carls
Hague 1928

White to play

White noticed a sacrifice, 1 ♖xd6 exd6 2 ♕xf6. He realized that he would immediately get one pawn for the Exchange and might add a second one via 3 ♖xd6 or 3 ♖d5/4 ♖b5.

The timing seems right. White's pieces are as aggressively placed as they are likely to be. If White plays something else, Black will be able to improve his position, say with ... ♘d7, and the chance for ♖xd6 is lost. That makes this a critical moment, right?

Well, not exactly. It's not clear that White would stand better after 1 ♖xd6 – that is, better than Black is in the 2 ♕xf6 position or better than White was before 1 ♖xd6. That indicates there is no real urgency.

White can improve his position in other ways, such as with 1 h4 and 2 h5. Then he might win by pushing the pawn to h6 or exchanging on g6. If he follows with an advance of the g-pawn, Black's king may be in serious trouble.

White added it all up and chose **1 h4!**. Black thwarted his plan with **1 ... h5**. But that made **2 ♖xd6!** much stronger than a move earlier.

After **2 ... exd6 3 ♕xf6** the defense 3 ... ♖d7 loses another pawn to 4 ♗d5 and ♕xg6+ (or 4 ... ♔h7 5 ♗xf7).

Also 3 ... ♖a6 4 ♗d5 ♔f8 is doomed by 5 ♖d3 followed by ♖f3 or ♖e3/♕h8 mate.

Instead, the game went **3 ... ♖f8 4 ♖xd6 ♕c5**.

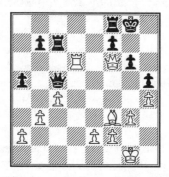

White to play

Now **5 ♗d5!** is a paralyzing shot that threatens 6 ♕xg6+ (thanks to 1 ... h5).

Black was forced into **5 ... ♔h7**. But that makes his king vulnerable to **6 g4!**, e.g. 6 ... hxg4? 7 h5 gxh5 8 ♕h6+ and 9 ♖g6 mate.

Black tried for counterplay with **6 ... ♕a3** but he was lost after **7 gxh5 ♕c1+ 8 ♔h2 ♕h6 9 ♗xf7!** and hxg6+.

Going back, we can see that 1 h4! gave Black an opportunity to lose quickly with 1 ... h5?. Better was 1 ... ♖c5, when White has to find another winning idea, such as 2 g4 followed by 3 g5 or 2 ♕d2 and 3 ♕h6 – or even 2 ♖xd6 after all. Nevertheless White had improved his chances over the immediate 1 ♖xd6.

Plus-moves

When a game ends in victory without a turning point it often has a decisive trend instead. A master sees trends that others don't. That is, a master is better at recognizing when one side's winning chances are gradually and steadily improving.

This is not a matter of calculation but rather visualization. The master sees the plus-moves that will improve a position.

Christiansen – Short, Hastings 1979/80: **1 d4 e6 2 c4 f5 3 g3 ♘f6 4 ♗g2 ♗b4+ 5 ♗d2 ♕e7 6 ♘f3 0-0 7 0-0 ♗xd2 8 ♘bxd2 d6 9 ♖e1 e5 10 e4**

Christiansen – Short
Hastings 1979/80

Black to play

White wants to open the center because of his superior development and because his rook is lined up against the Black queen, e.g. 10 ... exd4? 11 exf5 and 12 ♘xd4 with advantage.

Black is tempted to minimize the opening of lines with 10 ... f4 and 11 gxf4 exf4. But that still leaves White with opportunities to blow open the center with e4-e5 or c4-c5.

Black knew from his understanding of pawn structures that it would be much better if he could occupy f4 with a piece, ideally a knight, rather than a pawn. But that would take one and possibly two extra moves to execute and cost one and possibly two pawns.

So Black took a short look into the future, at **10 ... f4 11 gxf4 ♘h5!**. He saw **12 fxe5 ♘f4!** and then **13 exd6 cxd6**.

White to play

How do you evaluate such a position? There's too much to calculate to draw a definitive conclusion.

But Black can visualize. He can see that his position will improve once he carries out a series of obvious moves – ... ♘c6, ... ♗g4, ... ♖f6 and ... ♖af8.

97

This makes Black's position easier to play, and that's important, as we'll see in Chapter Seven. White could only stop these moves by changing the position sharply, say with 14 e5 – so that 14 ... ♘c6? 15 e6! and 16 d5. But Black should have strong attacking chances if he shifts his queen, say with 14 ... ♕f7 and 15 ... ♕g6.

White preferred **14 ♕b3 ♘c6 15 d5**. Black's attacking chances grew after **15 ... ♘e5 16 ♘xe5 dxe5 17 ♘f1 ♕h4 18 ♘g3 ♖f6 19 ♖e3 ♗h3**. He should have won in the complications that followed **20 ♘f5 ♖xf5! 21 exf5 ♗xg2**.

Black appreciated that he could create a good trend. But what do you do about a bad trend?

The first step is to visualize the near future. The second is to make sure it doesn't happen.

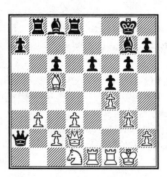

Short – Kasparov
Wijk aan Zee 2000

White to play

Black's pieces seem active enough to equalize. He has tactics such as 1 ♘c3 ♕a5! (2 b4 ♕a3) to annoy White.

But this is deceptive. The pawn structure favors White considerably. Black faces long-term problems defending the target at a7 and trying to find good squares for his bad c8-bishop.

In short, time is on White's side. He can play slowly, with **1 ♖f2**, to protect his queen so that it will be safe to continue 2 ♘c3. Unless something changes significantly, his pieces will improve. Black's won't.

For example, 1 ... ♗d7 2 ♘c3 ♕a5 3 ♘a4! ♕xd2 4 ♖xd2 is very good for White. After 4 ... ♖b7 5 ♗e7 ♖a8 6 ♗d6 and ♗e5 he is preparing to trade into a good-knight-vs.-bad-bishop ending in which he will double rooks on the a-file.

That's a trend Black knew he had to stop. He did it with **1 ... ♕a6 2 ♘c3**:

Black to play

And now **2 ... ⬛xb3!** followed by **3 cxb3 ⬛xd3** gave Black two pawns for the sacrificed Exchange.

In unbalanced material situations like that, it's the positional plusses that matter. So even though he seems to be ahead in material, Black will be worse in view of his bad bishop.

But he should be able to draw. That's what happened eventually after **4 ♕a2 ⬛xc3 5 b4 ⬛a3 6 ♕c2 ⬛d3 7 ⬛d2 ⬛d5! 8 ⬛xd5 cxd5 7 ♗f2 ♗b7**. Black saved the game because he realized in time that he was on the wrong side of a trend, and he took steps to change it.

The simplest way to detect a trend is to identify how many progress-making plus-moves each side can make in the near future. Consider this case:

Hasangatin – Yakovich
Krasnodar 2002

Black to play

This has all the footprints of a Sicilian Defense in which ... ♕a5 followed by ... b5-b4 provides Black with counterplay. But he has to be concerned about ♗h4 followed by ♗xf6.

Is Black willing to retake ... gxf6 ? Or give up a pawn (... ♗xf6/♕xd6)? Or meet ♗h4 with ... g5 ?

He can avoid all this with 1 ... ♘d7. That looks good because the knight can get back into play with tempo (... ♘c5).

But there's a drawback. Retreating the knight to d7 makes 2 ♘d5 attractive. That threatens 3 ♘xe7+ and 4 ♕xd6. And more significantly it enables White to recapture on d5 with a piece after ... ♗xd5, rather than a less desirable pawn.

So Black has to evaluate **1 ... ♘d7 2 ♘d5 ♗xd5 3 ♕xd5!**. That would leave him with a bad bishop on e7, while White enjoys a nice outpost on d5. Nevertheless, Black chose this and followed up with **3 ... ♖c6!**.

White to play

Black's 1 ... ♘d7 decision makes sense because he can improve his position with ... ♕c7 and ... ♖c8, followed by ... ♘b6 and ... ♘c4 or ... ♘a4, depending on what's available.

That makes four plus-moves that White can't easily stop. To figure out whether they amount to a significant trend, Black has to answer another question. Does White have plus-moves, and if so, how many?

The answer is: Not many. His king would be better off on b1. But his heavy pieces can't improve much. The only significant way to improve is by a knight maneuver, such as ♘d2-f1-e3.

This gives Black enough of a picture of the future to convince him that 1 ... ♘d7! was good. His judgment was confirmed when the game continued by **4 ♔b1 ♕c7 5 c3 ♖c8**.

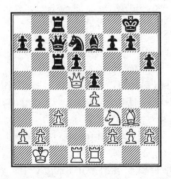

White to play

It should be easy to see that Black has made progress since the previous diagram. He would improve further if White began his knight maneuver, 6 ♘d2, because of 6 ... ♗g5!.

Then Black will try to trade bishop for knight and drop a knight on c4 with tempo, e.g. 7 ... ♘b6 8 ♕b3 ♗xd2 9 ♖xd2 ♘c4 and 10 ... ♖b6. White can avoid that with 7 ♘b3 but after 7 ... ♘b6 and 8 ... ♘c4 he is worse.

How did this happen to White? Simple. Black made progress and White didn't.

White avoided 6 ♘d2 and preferred **6 ♗h4 ♘b6 7 ♕d3**. But Black's attack has gained so much momentum that he could afford to weaken his kingside with **7 ... g5! 8 ♗g3 ♘a4**.

White to play

Black has ideas to work with such as a knight sacrifice on b2 or c3, as well as ... ♕b6, which threatens mate on b2 or a capture on c3. A typical winning line is 9 ♕c2 ♘xb2! 10 ♔xb2 ♖xc3 11 ♕a4 ♕c5 followed by ... ♖c6-b6+ or –a6.

White actually played **9 ♖e2** and **resigned** after **9 ... b5! 10 ♖c2 b4 11 ♕b5 ♘xb2!** in view of 12 ♖xb2 bxc3 13 ♖c2 ♖b6.

Visualize the Rooks

One of the tricks to spotting a potential trend is visualizing how the rooks will come into action. If one side can make much better use of his rooks and has a free hand to do it, that's usually a good trend.

In the Christiansen-Short game, Black's ability to play ... ♖f6 and ... ♖af8 indicated one. In Short-Kasparov, the possibility of White doubling rooks on the a-file, while Black's rooks had little to do, showed another. In Hasangatin-Yakovich, the tripling of Black's heavy pieces on the c-file – while White couldn't make his lazy rooks do significantly more – was also revealing. Here's one final example:

Nijboer – Rublevsky
Bled 2002

White to play

Each player has some good things to say about his position. If you can eliminate your opponent's assets, it leaves you with the only good pieces on the board.

White appreciated that Black's best piece was his bishop. Black, on the other hand, appreciated the need to eliminate one of White's best pieces, with 1 ... ♕g5. That threatens mate on g2 and would force a trade of queens.

White beat him to the punch with **1 ♗e4! ♗xe4 2 ♕xe4**. Black was worried about b3-b4, so he spent a tempo on **2 ... a5**, leaving us with another position to evaluate.

White to play

But this one is easier to judge. White has no open files for his rooks and no easy way of opening a file. However, he can greatly enhance his rooks with ♖ad1-d3-g3. That takes aim at White's best target, g7.

Black's rooks don't seem to have a future. He'd like to trade knights so he can play ... a4 but there is no easy way to force a swap.

We can carry the visualization a bit further. Black is bound to castle kingside. But that will make him vulnerable to a heavy piece attack of ♖g3/♕g4 along with ♘b2-d3-f4-h5.

White's pieces, particularly his rooks, have a future. This is another way of saying the future belongs to White. He made progress in the game: **3 ♖ad1 g6 4 ♖d3 ♔f8 5 ♖g3 ♔g7 6 h4 h5** and now **7 ♖g5! ♖a7 8 ♖d1!**.

102

The other rook is headed for either f3 or g3. Black was able to temporarily delay him with **8 ... ♕a8 9 ♕f4 ♕c6** but then came **10 ♖d3 ♖aa8 11 ♘b2 ♖h6 12 ♖f3**.

Black to play

It's far from the finish but the difference in rooks ensures that White will be the one making threats for the foreseeable future. The beginning of the end was **12 ... ♖f8 13 ♕d2 ♕e4 14 ♘d3 ♖a8** (not 14 ... ♕xh4? 15 ♖f4 ♕xg5 16 ♖xf7+ and ♕xg5).

Then came **15 ♖gg3 ♖f8** (here 15 ... ♘xe5? loses a piece to 16 ♖f4) **16 ♕g5 ♖h7 17 ♕e7 ♕c6 18 ♖xg6+! ♔h8** (18 ... ♔xg6 19 ♕g5 mate) **19 ♖gf6! ♖g7 20 ♖h6+ ♔g8 21 ♖g3! resigns**.

Of course, other pieces can improve their positions in the middlegame or early ending. But it is often easier to visualize the bettering of the rooks on each side. And since rooks are the second-most powerful pieces, and the ones that improve the most after move 10, it pays to pay extra attention to them.

Time for some quiz positions:

Quiz

26

Nevostrujev – Volzhin

Tomsk 2001

White to play

Who does time favor and what should White do?

27
Carlsen – Nakamura
Wijk aan Zee 2011

White to play

White wants to push his g-pawn but preparation is in order. He might consider 1 ♕e3, followed by 2 ♕g3. Or perhaps or 1 ♘d4 or 1 ♖dg1. What else?

28
Foisor – Thanh
Khanty-Mansiysk 2010

Black to play

Is time on Black's side and what can she do?

29
Seirawan – van der Wiel
Wijk aan Zee 1983

White to play

White seems to have a lead in development but 1 d3 or 1 f4 doesn't exploit it. Any other ideas?

30
Atalik – Negelescu
Rumania 2003

White to play

What should White do?

31
Karpov – Yusupov
London 1989

White to play

Black's last two moves were ... ♖d5 and ... ♛h4. What does that mean to White?

Chapter Six:
Winnability

Any experienced player can figure out when he has an advantage, particularly a big advantage. A master knows when his advantage is big *enough*.

Enough to win. When a position is that good, a master knows that he doesn't have to look for elaborate plans or to calculate risk-taking variations. He should be able to win with relatively simple moves, especially one-move and two-move threats, and simple precautions to eliminate counterplay.

McShane – So
Wijk aan Zee 2011

Black to play

After the game, White was surprised to find that his computer claimed he was only slightly better here. He knew the evaluation must be wrong. Black's weak king is what matters most, by far.

Aside from the immediate threat of ♕xh6, White can make solid progress with straightforward ideas such as ♖c5-e5 followed by ♖e7 or ♖e6. Once his rook penetrates, Black's situation should be hopeless.

Black understood this, too, so he seized the initiative with **1 ... ♖d7 2 ♕xh6 ♖g7**, threatening mate on g2. Then came **3 g3 ♕d4**, with another threat, 4 ... ♖xg3+.

However, it should be easy to see that White doesn't have enough weaknesses to enable Black to keep making threats. Black, on the other hand, has plenty of weaknesses and that's why White has a won game.

After a brief period of defense, **4 ♕e6+ ♖f7 5 ♕e2 ♔g7 6 ♖f1**, he was ready to consolidate with ♔g2 and regain the initiative.

This happened quickly because **6 ... ♔g6** allowed him to substitute for ♔g2 with **7 ♖d1!**.

Black to play

White would win after 7 ... ♖xf2? 8 ♕e8+!. Black had to pull back and resignation was getting closer after **7 ... ♕f6 8 ♕e3 b6 9 ♖d4! ♖e7 10 ♕d3+ ♔g7 11 ♖f4**.

This was more than a case of 'just moving around' in a superior position. White had a general plan of getting his rook closer to the Black king, ideally to g5.

In fact, **Black resigned** after **11 ... ♕e6 12 ♖f5 ♖f7**, when he realized that two precise moves, **13 ♖g5+! ♔h6 14 ♕d1!**, would make resistance futile.

A master is able to win more often because he has a better understanding of what it takes to win. He sees winning potential in positions that other players – even computers – think are only mildly favorable. A master also rejects moves that lead to positions that are favorable – but not favorable *enough*.

Most of all, a master has a better sense of when to trade pieces when he has an advantage. This is critical when a player faces a choice of whether to liquidate a very good position or press for a better one.

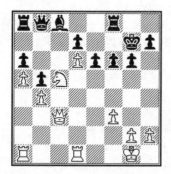

Kovalev – Kuznetsov
Alushta 2004

White to play

White has what annotators like to call a queenside bind. It's not a winning position and there are no indefensible Black weaknesses. White's pieces are simply much better placed than Black's.

But there's some urgency. Black can unravel by means of ... ♖f7 and ... ♗b7. Then he threatens to consolidate with ... ♗d5 and even grab a second pawn, ... ♕xd6. Given time, Black is winning.

White can foil that by taking the bishop on b7 and penetrating at c7 with his heavy pieces. For example, **1 ♖ac1** is an obvious candidate. Black could begin the unraveling with **1 ... ♖f7** and then **2 ♕e3 ♗b7**.

A bit of inspection shows that White can't improve his position further with quiet moves. This means **3 ♘xb7! ♕xb7 4 ♖c7** makes sense. After **4 ... ♕b8**:

White to play

Once again there are obvious candidates. One is 5 ♖dc1 so that if Black tries to activate his pieces (5 ... ♕e8 followed by ... e5, ... ♕e6 and ... ♖ff8) he can continue 6 ♖b7 and ♖cc7 with great pressure.

Or White can try to force a winning endgame with 5 ♕b6, followed by ♖dc1 and then ♖b7 or ♕xb8/♖a7.

Each of these lines looks very good for him and he would likely end up a pawn or so ahead in an endgame. But is it good *enough*?

Maybe not. As promising as these lines are, a master would be at least a little apprehensive about heading into a mere pawn-up endgame.

Why? Because White's earlier position was simply too good to sell cheaply. It was the kind of position you can win in the middlegame.

White wanted more than an endgame and found it on the kingside. Back at the first diagram he detected a target at f6 and played **1 g4!**. His idea is 2 g5 followed by 3 gxf6+ ♖xf6? 4 ♘e4, winning.

Black's queenside pieces can't defend the king and he was in deep trouble after **1 ... g5 2 h4!**.

Black to play

Black was lost after **2 ... gxh4? 3 g5** because of **3 ... ♖f7 4 gxf6+ ♔f8** and then **5 ♔f2 ♗b7 6 ♕e3**, with killing ideas of ♕g5/♖g1/♕g8 mate and ♕h6+/♖d4/♖g1-g8 mate.

Yes, Black could have defended better. But even after **2 ... h6** White would have somewhat better chances – with **3 ♖a2** followed by ♖h2, ♔g2 and ♖dh1, for instance – than if he had tried to win on the queenside with **1 ♖ac1** and ♘xb7.

Winnability

How does a master assess winnability? There are several factors including (a) the material situation, (b) the positional plusses and (c) how close the position is to an endgame.

If it's pretty close – so that a trade of one pair of pieces will reach a bookish endgame position – then experience or textbook learning should give you a fairly accurate evaluation. This is where knowing basic endgame principles will count.

Leko – San Segundo
Moscow 1994

White to play

Black has just offered a trade of queens with ... ♕d5. Should White accept the invitation?

To be absolutely certain about the wisdom of **1 ♕xd5** you'd have to know some subtle endgame theory.

You would know that White has excellent chances in a rook ending if his extra pawn were a b-pawn. But with an a-pawn, theory says Black would have to make some serious errors to lose.

However, you don't have to memorize pages of book. A master would recognize that any endgame like this – with a single, extra pawn that is passed and on the queenside – is difficult to win when White's rook is in front of, rather than behind, the pawn. That would tell White to avoid **1 ♕xd5?**.

He played **1 ♕f4!**. This (a) avoids the drawish rook endgame, (b) protects the only potential target for Black and (c), watches his own target at f7 (**1 ... ♕b5?? 2 ♕xf7+**).

After Black replied **1 ... ♔g8**, White connected his heavy pieces, **2 ♖f6**. Then came **2 ... ♔g7 3 a6 ♖d7**.

109

White to play

It might seem that White was thinking: "I'll attack f7 and push the a-pawn to distract him enough to win the f-pawn."

But that wasn't his idea. His goal was to improve the position of his rook and he succeeded so well that he has virtually a forced win beginning with **4 ♕f3!**.

The point is that now a queen trade is very good because White can get his rook behind the a-pawn. For example, 4 ... ♕xf3 5 ♖xf3 ♖d2 threatens 6 ... ♖a2!, which would draw.

But it can be met by 6 ♖a3!, since Black loses immediately after 6 ... ♖xf2+? 7 ♔g1 and 8 a7.

In the game, Black met 4 ♕f3 with **4 ... ♕c5**. But then **5 ♖c6!** threatened both the queen and a mate, 6 ♕f6+ or 6 ♕c3+ followed by ♖c8.

The game, which seemed drawish a few moves ago, was over immediately: **5 ... ♕d4 6 ♕c3! ♕xc3 7 ♖xc3 ♖d2 8 ♖a3! resigns**.

What clinched victory was realizing how winnable the rook ending is once White's rook gets behind the passed pawn. It didn't take lengthy calculation or memorization of book positions. It was knowing the behind-the-pawn principle.

The vast amount of endgame theory concerns specific positions in which one side has an extra pawn. The variations are often staggeringly difficult. But what's more important is to know the general cases: When is an extra pawn enough to win? When is a second extra pawn needed? What are the winning piece-vs.-piece matchups?

Here's another example.

Kramnik – Svidler
Linares 1999

White to play

Black has only a pawn for the Exchange. But White lacks a pawn that could he could try to queen. Take everything off the board but the pawns, the kings and a White rook and Black bishop, and it's a possible draw.

Yet Black resigned in six moves. White accomplished that due to two factors. The first was his tactical vision. He saw that the 'impossible' 1 ♗xf7 was possible.

After Black captures the bishop, 2 ♕xd7! will work. Then 2 ... ♖xd7 leads to an endgame in which White has two rooks to battle the Black queen, with an equal number of pawns.

But calculation is only as good as the evaluation that accompanies it. The second factor that won the game was White's realization that the endgame is a win, in a fact a relatively easy one. Play went **1 ♗xf7! ♖xf7 2 ♕xd7 ♖xd7 3 ♖xd7+ ♔h6 4 ♖xc7**.

Black to play

White aimed for this because he knew the general case: Barring a complicating factor, two rooks beat a queen if pawns are equal.

The winning plan is elementary: The rooks will double up on the a-pawn and win it. After that, they can pick off the kingside pawns in the same way.

Black made it easy by playing **4 ... ♕d3**, hoping for 5 ♖a1 ♕d4! 6 ♖axa7 ♕xf2, with a likely draw because of Black's prospects for perpetual check.

But after **5 ♔g1!** it was safe for White's rooks to win the a-pawn. It was too late for Black to push it (5 ... a5 6 ♖a1 a4 7 ♖a7!, not 7 ♖xa4?? ♕d1+).

Black resigned after **5 ... ♕d4 6 ♖c2** in view of, say, 6 ... ♕a4 7 ♖cc1 a5 8 ♖a1 ♕b4 9 ♖a2! and 10 ♖fa1.

The Necessary 'How'

Another important factor in assessing whether a position is favorable enough is simply whether you can imagine how it would be won. But 'imagine' isn't the right word. Imagination has little to do with it. It's a matter of visualizing a plan.

Polovodin – Tseitlin
Leningrad 1985

White to play

White's last moves were ♗e3-f2 and the maneuver of his knight from c2 to f3. If his moves were words, they would say, "I'm going to win the h4-pawn."

But Black has a defense, 1 ... ♔g7 and 2 ... ♖h8. Does White have another plan?

Yes, he can go after the pawn immediately, with 1 ♘g5 and 2 ♗xh4. Then Black doesn't have time to play ... ♖h8.

But 1 ♘g5 is a big step because 1 ... ♗xg5 2 fxg5 creates bishops of opposite color. That might draw in an endgame, and Black can get closer to an ending with 2 ... ♖e8 and ... ♖xe1+.

That makes the position in the diagram a critical moment. By playing 1 ♘g5 White might either be throwing away a very favorable position or nailing down a win.

White figured out 1 ♘g5 ♗xg5 would be a win. And it had nothing to do with an extra pawn. He can visualize – without calculating – that once Black has no dark-squared bishop, he is highly vulnerable to mating threats on the long diagonal. White can't be sure – without calculating a lot – that it will be a forced win. But the visualization tells him it should be close to a win.

With that in mind, play went **1 ♘g5! ♗xg5 2 fxg5** and **2 ... ♖e8 3 ♗d4**.

Black to play

What White had visualized, when he looked at 1 ♘g5, were knockout plans. One goes ♗f6 followed by ♕f2 and ♕xh4-h8 mate. A similar one is c3-c4/♗c3 and ♕d4.

Now that the position has clarified he can calculate specific variations. A simple one runs 3 ... ♖xe1+? 4 ♕xe1 ♕xg5?? 5 ♕e8+ and 6 ♕h8 mate.

A better defense is 3 ... ♕d7 or 3 ... ♔f8, hoping to flee with the king. But calculation shows that 3 ... ♕d7 4 ♕f2 ♔f8 loses to 5 ♕xh4, e.g. 5 ... ♖xe1+ 6 ♕xe1 ♕a4 7 ♔h2 (7 ... ♕xa2? 8 ♗f6 and 9 ♕e7+ or 7 ... ♕c2 8 ♕h4).

In the game Black set a trap with **3 ... ♗e4**. He is hoping for 4 ♕f4? ♗xg2+! 5 ♔xg2 ♖xe1 6 ♕xh4 ♖e5!.

But once you have a positionally won game – and this is what one looks like – you don't need ingenuity. Precaution is usually enough. After White played **4 c4**, Black found **4 ... c5** in a bid to discourage ♕d4.

However, White can turn to another winning plan, with **5 ♗c3** and then **5 ... ♕d7 6 ♔g1** to stop ... ♕xh3+.

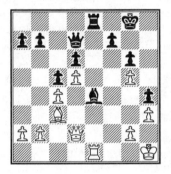

Black to play

Black had run out of good defensive tries (6 ... ♕f5 7 ♖f1 ♕d7 8 ♕f4 and wins) and the game ended with **6 ... b5 7 ♕f4 b4 8 ♗f6 ♗xg2 9 ♕xh4! ♖xe1+ 10 ♔xg2! ♖e2+ 11 ♔g1 resigns**.

'Positionally won game' is a useful cliché for annotators. But it means more to a master. When he can say with confidence that he has one, he knows it can be finished off with fairly simple, direct moves. He doesn't have to do a lot to win. The game is already won.

A position that is merely very favorable isn't in this category. It will require precision, not just precaution, as in the next example.

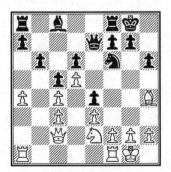

Bagirov – Kuzmin
Baku 1977

Black to play

Black sees that he has the advantage because the weakest target on the board lies at c4. If he gets to play ... ♗xc4, White will not only be a pawn down, but his d-pawn is probably doomed and his light squares may be fatally exposed. If that's not a 'positionally lost game', it's something very close to it.

A quick glance shows that if Black plays 1 ... ♗a6, White can defend c4 with his queen. If White's bishop were, say on d2 or a3, Black could carry out a simple maneuver, ... ♘d7-e5, take on c4 and win fairly easily.

But the bishop is on h4. The difference is that 1 ... ♗a6? is actually an error. White can insert 2 ♗xf6! and, following 2 ... ♕xf6, he can play 3 ♕b3 and bring his knight to life at g3. Black will still be better. But it's clearly not a positionally won game.

That prompted Black to make a no-turning-back decision, similar to 1 ♘g5! in the previous game. He played **1 ... g5!** and then **2 ♗g3 ♗a6**.

Yes, Black's king position is loosened. But White is tied to the defense of c4 and can't exploit the kingside. In fact after **3 ♕a2 ♘h5!** it is Black who has the more ominous threat on that wing of ... f7-f5-f4.

White to play

This is getting very close to positionally won territory. Play went **4 ♘c1 f5 5 ♕e2 ♕f7!**.

The threat of ... f4-f3 is immediate. The tactical justification for Black's play is that 6 ♗xd6? ♖fd8 7 ♗e5 ♖xd5 wins quickly.

White played **6 f4** and allowed the position to be opened, **6 ... exf3 7 ♖xf3 ♕g6 8 a5 f4! 9 exf4 gxf4**, now we've reached the positionally won stage.

That means Black can rely on fairly routine moves. The rest was **10 ♗f2 ♖ae8 11 ♕f1 ♖e4 12 axb6 ♗xc4 13 ♕d1 axb6 14 ♖a4 b5 15 ♖a6 ♖e5! 16 ♗xc5 ♖fe8!** (intending ... ♖e1+) **17 ♔f2 ♖e1 18 ♖xd6 ♕c2+!** in view of 19 ♕xc2 ♖f1 mate. A little extra care – evaluating the consequences of 1 ... g5 – made a huge difference.

To win a won game you typically need a 'how'. It could be a general plan like Black's kingside advance in the last example or more specific like the mate-on-the-long-diagonal theme of the previous one.

Without a 'how', even a position that seems hugely advantageous may not be winnable. Here's a striking example.

114

Kramnik – Zviagintsev
Moscow 2005

White to play

White enjoys iron control of the c-file and a considerable advantage in operating room. There is no Black counterplay. All the ingredients seem in place for a slow, plodding win by a world champion.

Except ... White lacks a plan. He can't improve his position through simple means. He couldn't find a way to make a6 or b6 into a target. Just moving the furniture around aimlessly won't do the job.

The game ended in a draw after a series of quiet moves, beginning with **1 ♗f1 ♘e8 2 ♖7c3 ♕d8 3 ♕d2 ♘f6 4 ♖c7 ♘e8 5 ♖7c3 ♘f6 8 ♖c7 ♘e8.** White had no 'how'.

Golden Rule

There's a golden rule about converting an advantage that most non-masters don't appreciate. They don't appreciate it because they simply don't believe it:

It is usually easier to win with a substantial *positional* advantage than with an equally substantial *material* advantage.

Amateurs don't believe it because they exaggerate the significance of material. After all, they can see an extra pawn. A positional advantage is harder to detect. As a result they have a difficult time believing the rule in positions like the following.

Cebalo – Smirin
Solin 1999

White to play

Most players would try to solve this as a 'White to play and win' with calculation. Some will see that 1 ♕c7 looks good. Others will notice that Black can save himself with 1 ... ♕e6 because 2 d7? ♕xd5 threatens mate on g2.

And many will conclude that the solution is easy because 1 ♖xh5+ wins a pawn. There is only one variation to look at and it runs 1 ... gxh5 2 ♕xh5+ ♔g7 3 ♕xe2. The forcing moves end with 3 ... ♕xd6+ 4 ♔h1.

But the experienced player is suspicious of this. It's not the variation he doubts but the evaluation. At the end, after 4 ♔h1, White has no passed pawn. His does have an extra pawn but it's located on the kingside. If White does win, the 'how' – promoting the h-pawn – will take a lot of moves and thinking.

Instead, he played the superior **1 ♖e5**. The main point is that 1 ... ♖xe5 2 ♕xe5 enables White to break the blockade at d7 with ♕e7!.

Black's best was 1 ... ♖d2, so he can meet 2 ♖e7? with 2 ... ♕xd6+ 3 ♕xd6 ♖xd6 4 ♖xf7+ ♔h6 with a dead draw.

But **1 ... ♖d2** allows a better version of the combination, **2 ♖xh5+! gxh5 3 ♕xh5+ ♔g8 4 ♕g5+ ♔f8 5 ♕xd2.**

Black to play

Why is this an easier win? It's not because White has two extra pawns, rather than the one he'd have after 1 ♖xh5+?.

No, what matters most is that he kept his d-pawn. That means he can break the blockade or force a trade of queens after ♕d4-c5-c7. The 'how' is much easier this time. (In fact, the fastest way to win in the first diagram is 1 ♕d4!. That makes 2 ♖e5 a powerful winning idea now that 2 ... ♖d2 is not possible.)

Note that what mattered was a passed pawn, not necessarily an *extra* pawn. Good defenders understand that, too. Let's see how both White and Black used the golden rule in the following example.

Kramnik – Aronian
Dortmund 2006

Black to play

White's obvious threat is to take the e7-pawn. His less obvious one is to dominate the c-file by doubling rooks. Black can foil both threats with a gain of time, 1 ... f6, and then 2 ... ♖c8 or 2 ... ♖c7.

But that creates an ugly hole at e6. White can try to exploit it, after 2 ♗e3 or 2 ♗d2, with ♕e4-e6+ followed by f3-f4-f5, or ♖e1 or h2-h4-h5. With a positional, rather than material advantage, White has an easier 'how'.

Black chose **1 ... ♖c7!** because he understood that after 2 ♗xe7 ♖fc8 or 2 ... ♖e8 (3 ♗xd6 ♖xc1 4 ♗xb8 ♖xd1+) he has improved the power of his pieces, a positional gain for him. White has made a material gain. But his extra pawn means little because it is a doubled f-pawn.

White also understood this and replied **2 ♖c6!**. He threatens to take on a6, a much more valuable pawn because White would likely be able to create a passed a-pawn. Black replied **2 ... ♖xc6 3 dxc6 ♖c8**.

White to play

Once again White can win a pawn, with 4 ♗xe7 ♖xc6 and now 5 ♕e4!. The tactical point is that 5 ... ♕c7 allows 6 ♖xd6! ♖xd6 7 ♕a8+ (7 ... ♗f8?? 8 ♕xf8 mate).

Better is 5 ... ♕c8 and then 6 ♖xd6 ♖xd6 7 ♗xd6 leaves White with another pawn-up endgame. But it will be very hard to win, perhaps impossible against the best defense.

117

This explains why he preferred **4 ♖c1!**. The protected passed pawn is much stronger than an extra doubled pawn. Play went **4 ... e6 5 ♗d2 ♕c7**.

If there were no queenside pawns, White would be able to break the blockade at c7 by means of ♕a4 and ♗a5 or ♕b4-b7.

But as it stands, he was able to make progress with **6 a4!** and then **6 ... d5 7 axb5 axb5 8 ♕b4 ♖b8 9 ♕a3! ♗d4 10 ♕a6 ♗e5 11 f4 ♗d6 12 ♗a5 ♕c8 13 ♕a7! ♖a8 14 ♕b6 ♖b8 15 ♕d4**.

Black to play

White will win because he can push the c-pawn or win the Black b-pawn. For example, 15 ... ♗c7 16 ♗xc7 ♕xc7 17 ♖c5 and ♕b4.

Black preferred **15 ... b4** but then came **16 c7**. White would win after 16 ... ♖b7 17 ♕f6! ♗xc7 18 ♕e5!. Instead, the game ended with **16 ... ♖a8 17 ♕b6 ♗f8 18 ♗xb4 ♗xb4 19 ♕xb4 ♕e8** and **Black resigned** before ♕b7 and the advance of the b and c-pawns.

Positional, Not Material

There are many, many examples of that: A passed pawn – a positional advantage – turns out to be superior to an extra pawn – a material advantage. Yet the golden rule is difficult for many amateurs to accept. Part of the reason is that they're confused by the somewhat vague, somewhat imposing word 'positional'. If we replaced it with 'non-material' they'd have an easier time grasping positions like the following.

Rubinstein – Tarrasch
Carlsbad 1923

White to play

White has a big positional – sorry, a big 'non-material' – edge because of his superiority on light squares. A master sitting in White's chair will try shifting his pieces around and around because it's so hard for Black to defend h7 and g8.

He doesn't have to calculate long variations to determine whether there is a forced win. He feels there is a *likely* win. As long as he can keep making credible threats, that's enough for him to continue with confidence.

White began with **1 ♕d5**. He threatens 2 ♕xe5, of course. But his main idea is 2 ♕f7! followed by a decisive check (or a mate) on the eighth rank.

Black's difficulties are illustrated by **1 ... ♕f6**. This natural move meets both threats but leaves the knight unprotected. White would reply **2 ♕b5!**, with two new threats, 2 ♕xb8+ and 2 ♕e8+.

Black could meet one of them with **2 ... ♕e6+**. But then comes **3 g4**.

Black to play

The attacked knight is lost after 3 ... ♘d7 4 ♗f5 or 3 ... ♘a6 4 ♗f5 (4 ... ♕f6 or 4 ... ♕d6 allow 5 ♕e8+).

That leaves 3 ... ♕c8, abandoning a pawn, 4 ♕xe5. White would then be close to a forced win and can finish off immediately after 4 ... ♘d7? 5 ♕f5 and 4 ... ♘c6? 5 ♕c5.

Black avoided this fate by choosing **1 ... ♕c7** instead of 1 ... ♕f6 back at the previous diagram. He protects his knight and e-pawn this way but leaves the kingside vulnerable to ♕e6-g6-h7 mate.

White prepared that with **2 ♗f5!**. He needs to do that because the immediate 2 ♕e6 allows 2 ... ♕d7!, trading queens and fleeing into a likely draw.

Black found a defense in **2 ... ♘c6**. His idea is to meet 3 ♕e6 with 3 ... ♘e7 4 ♕f7 ♕d8, when everything is, at least temporarily, covered.

White to play

But with such a huge positional edge – those light squares! – White should be able to make progress with simple threats. The one he chose was **3 ♕c4!**.

He threatens to win the knight with ♗e4 (once he rules out ... ♕d7+ with 4 g4!).

Black would lose after the weakening 3 ... h5 because of 4 ♕e6 ♘e7 5 ♕f7! and ♕xh5+ or ♕f8+.

Black tried **3 ... ♕d6** but then came **4 ♕f7!**. Black could have resigned in view of 4 ... ♕f6 5 ♕e8+ or 4 ... ♘e7 5 ♕f8+. But he waited until after **4 ... ♕d8 5 ♕g6!**.

If you looked up that game, you'd find another instructive point. Just before 1 ♕d5, White swapped a pair of rooks. He did it because without a rook, Black's first rank became vulnerable to mates.

But usually the player with a positional – as opposed to material – advantage, will avoid trades. A master would know, for instance, that a trade of either the rooks or queens would vaporize White's winning chances in the following position.

Mikenas – Sliwa
Riga 1959

White to play

White controls more space. What 'controls more space' really means is that White can put his pieces safely on a lot more squares than Black. Most of those squares are on the kingside, where ... h6 is a slight weakening.

It's true that White has weaker pawns than Black, at a2 and c4. But, one more time, a king counts *more*. From experience White knew that the most important factor in a heavy-piece ending is king vulnerability.

Therefore, White's non-material advantage means his best winning chance lies in a kingside attack, beginning with **1 ♖d4! ♖c8 2 h4!**.

White uses his rook to defend his c-pawn, maintain control of the d-file and prepare for an assault on g7. He followed this with a luft-move that is also invaluable to his attack. Then came **2 ... ♕c7 3 ♕g3**.

White to play

Only two and a half moves have been played since the previous diagram but White's winning chances are much more visible. He will play ♖g4 and meet ... g6 with h4-h5. One way or another, the kingside will be opened up.

Black's problems aren't solved by 3 ... f5, for example, because White can build up with ♔h2, f2-f4, h4-h5, ♕g6 and ♖d6.

He made a different concession, **3 ... h5.** The pawn can't last long on h5. After 4 ♕g5 g6 White could blast open the kingside with 5 g4 hxg4 6 ♖xg4 and 7 h5.

Instead, Black sought counterplay on the other wing, and the game went **4 ♕g5 ♕c5 5 ♖f4 ♕a3** and then **6 ♔h2 ♕xa2 7 ♕xh5 ♖f8 8 ♕d1 ♕a5 9 ♕e2 ♖d8**.

White to play

The most natural way of continuing is to advance his pawn to h5 and double the heavy pieces against g7. This takes a while to execute but Black found no defense. The game went **10 h5! ♕d2 11 ♕g4 ♕e1 12 ♕g5 ♖d1 13 ♖g4 ♕g1+ 14 ♔g3 g6 15 hxg6** and **White won**.

Material Imbalance

When material is not equal but only slightly out of balance, positional advantages usually decide the outcome. This is most evident when a player gives up the Exchange for one or two pawns.

If it's a difference of one pawn, the player with the rook is marginally ahead. If it's two pawns, the other player holds an equally small edge. In either case, the edge may not be enough to win without positional plusses. Few people understood that better than the sixth world champion, Mikhail Botvinnik.

Botvinnik – Lundin
Stockholm 1962

White to play

White's previous moves were designed to grab on e4. But he can't keep an extra pawn because after 1 ♗xe4 Black will reply 1 ... ♗h3, threatening both 1 ... ♗xf1 and 1 ... ♖xe4.

White does have a defense to both threats, 2 ♗g2. But then 2 ... ♛xd1 3 ♖xd1 ♗xg2 and 4 ... ♖xe2 reestablishes material equality.

So this amounts to a critical moment. White has to decide whether he has good winning chances after 4 ♘xg2 ♖xe2 5 ♖d7. Sure, he has the better position but is it enough?

Botvinnik saw a way to get a much more significant positional advantage by creating slight material imbalance. He played **1 ♗xe4 ♗h3 2 ♛c2!** and then **2 ... ♗xf1 3 ♔xf1**.

Black to play

White is certain to win a second pawn, at h7 or b7. But what is much more important is that by eliminating Black's bishop, he dominates the light squares. Black will be unable to use his rooks because he has to worry about kingside mating threats directed at the h7 target.

Black found the best defense, **3 ... ♘d6 4 ♗xd6 ♕xd6**. That gave White a choice of which pawn to capture. A good argument can be made in favor 5 ♗xb7 ♖ab8 6 ♗c6 followed by 7 a4, to keep his two extra pawns.

But that still leaves the 'how' question. Creating a passed pawn on the queenside doesn't seem possible.

That's why White chose **5 ♗xh7!** and then **5 ... ♖ad8 6 ♘f3**.

Black to play

This is easier to win because of the inability of Black's rooks and bishop to defend his light-square weaknesses, such as at g6 and h7. For example, 6 ... ♕xa3? allows 7 ♗g6 and ♕f5 or 7 ♕f5 followed by 8 ♕h5 with a threat of ♗g6+.

Aside from tactics like that, White has a totally riskless winning plan of pushing the e-pawn. This unfolded with **6 ... ♖f8 7 ♗g6 ♕e6** (otherwise 8 ♕f5! wins).

Once again we see how the absence of counterplay allows a player to take his time. White played **8 ♔g2** and then **8 ... ♖d5 9 e4! ♖d6 10 ♖b4!**.

He is beginning to make game-winning threats, such as 11 e5 ♗xe5 12 ♖h4+ ♔g8 13 ♗h7+ ♔f7 14 ♘g5+.

Black struggled on with **10 ... ♗e7 11 ♗f5 ♕h6**.

White to play

White's positional edge has grown so great that he has an alternate winning idea, 12 ♕xc7 ♗d8 13 ♕xb7 followed by creating a passed queenside pawn.

He preferred **12 ♖c4 ♗d8 13 e5 ♖d5 14 ♘h4! ♖d2 15 ♕c3** and then **15 ... ♔g8 16 ♖f4 ♖d5 17 ♕f3! resigns** (in view of 18 ♕xd5+ or 18 ♗h7+/♖xf8).

Many players think that the best way to learn what it takes to win a game is to lock themselves in a room with endgame books. Bad idea.

Better idea: Find games in which one side wins after creating a slight material imbalance, like Exchange-for-pawn. These games, if they're not just sacrificial mating attacks, will underline the importance of positional advantages. Some databases will allow you find lots of games like that. They should be excellent study material.

The Winning Hierarchy

The corollary of what we said earlier – that a master is reluctant to trade pieces when he has a positional edge – is that a master is usually eager to trade pieces when he has a material edge. But which pieces?

If you are only one pawn ahead, which pieces do you want to keep? If you trade all the pieces and get down to just kings and pawns, you have excellent winning chances. But for other matchups it's not that easy.

For masters it is. They know the winning hierarchy. Here's the list for pawn-up endgames. The most winnable endings are at the top, and they go in descending order to the hardest at the bottom:

King-vs.-king endings

Knight-vs.-knight endings

Queen-vs.-queen endings

Bishop-vs.-bishop (same color) endings

Bishop-vs.-knight endings

Knight-vs.-bishop endings

Rook-vs.-rook endings

Opposite colored bishop-vs.-bishop endings

This works best with positions in which one side has an extra pawn on the other wing, typically the queenside. If all the pawns are on the kingside, the hierarchy changes slightly. Knight-vs.-bishop moves higher up the list and bishop-vs.-knight moves well down.

Relatively inexperienced players are unaware of the hierarchy. This is true even of young, highly rated players.

During a session of the U.S. Chess School a few years ago, eight promising youngsters were asked to evaluate the winning chances of some of these matchups. They were given a slightly different example, with all the pawns on one wing:

Suppose all the pawns were on the kingside, with one player having pawns on the e-, f- g-, and h-files, and the other player having pawns just on the f-, g- and h- files. What are the winning chances, from zero to 100 percent, for each matchup?

The youngsters, almost all of whom soon became strong masters, gave varied answers. For example, with just rooks on the board, one student thought the right answer was zero, that is, no chance of winning. Another said the chances were only 10 percent. The right answer is more like a 30 percent.

All but one of the students thought that with same-colored bishops, the pawn-up player had reasonable winning chances, 40 or 50 percent. Their instructor, GM Joel Benjamin, told them it was really only about 20 percent.

And what about queen endings? Three of the eight students thought they offered a 20 or 30 percent chance of winning. It's more like 50 percent.

Even many experienced players have an irrational fear of queen endings, for example. Given a choice of what to swap in a pawn-up ♕+♗-vs.- ♕+♘ ending, they'll trade queens instead of minor pieces. That's often a blunder.

Gelfand – M. Gurevich
Linares 1991

Black to play

Queen endings are among the easiest to win. Yuri Averbakh, the great endgame authority, claimed they are even easier to win than knight endings. Here, for instance, **1 ... ♗xd4!** reaches either a won pawn ending or a won queen ending.

The pawn ending comes about from 2 ♕xd4 ♕b1+ 3 ♔g2 ♕e4+! 4 ♕xe4 fxe4. It takes longer to win after 4 f3 ♕xd4 5 exd4 ♔g5 6 f4+ ♔f6 but it is still a win.

The queen ending is won because Black can create an outside passed d-pawn after **2 exd4 ♕b2 3 ♔g2 e5 4 dxe5 ♕xe5**.

The winning technique is essentially the same with other same-piece endings. The superior side first forces the enemy to take steps to stop the passed pawn's advance. Then he advances his king and looks for an opportunity to raid pawns on the other wing.

White to play

In this case the first step was accomplished by **5 ♕d2+ ♔g7 6 f3 d4 7 ♔f2 ♕c5 8 ♕b2**. The second was realized by **8 ... ♔f6 9 ♔e2 ♕c4+ 10 ♔d2 ♔g5**.

The game ended with **11 ♕a3 ♕e6! 12 ♕b4 ♕e3+ 13 ♔c2 ♕f2+ 14 ♔c1 ♕g1+ 15 ♔c2 ♕xh2+ 16 ♔d3 ♕xg3 17 ♕e7+ ♔h6**.

When material is equal, positional plusses naturally take center stage. But the hierarchy continues to play a role. In the next example, Black has a positional edge in view of his passed h-pawn and White's doubled pawns. The hierarchy indicates he should have good winning chances. Let's see how two of the world's greatest endgame players handled it.

Portisch – Karpov
Tilburg 1986

Black to play

White naturally wants to liquidate the queenside pawns. Black can meet his threat of axb6 by offering either of two trades, 1 ... ♗d4 and 1 ... bxa5 2 ♗xa7 ♖b4.

The hierarchy gives an indication of which is correct. Black confirmed this by examining 1 ... ♗d4? and seeing that 2 ♗xd4 ♖xd4 is drawish, e.g. 3 ♖c1 ♔e7 (else 4 ♖c7+) 4 axb6 axb6 5 ♖h1 ♖d6 6 ♖h5.

The alternative was **1 ... bxa5 2 ♗xa7** and then **2 ... ♖b4! 3 ♖xb4 axb4**. This should be winnable because of three factors: First, Black has two passed pawns. Second, he can slow the advance of White's pawn (4 b6 ♗d4!). And third, the White f-pawns interfere with his bishop's ability to stop the h-pawn.

Play went **4 ♔e3 ♗e7 5 ♔d4 h5! 6 b6 b3 7 b7 ♗d6**.

126

White to play

Here 8 b8(♕) ♗xb8 9 ♗xb8 b2 is plainly lost. Ditto 8 ♔c3 h4 and ... h3.

There are a lot of other finesses to appreciate in this game, such as White's attempts to divert Black's bishop from control of b8, and Black's skillful use of his passed pawns. But that's not rare in bishop endgames. That's why they are winnable more often than rook endings.

Play went **8 ♔c3 h4 9 ♗d4! ♗b8!**. Black's point is that 9 ... h3? 10 ♗e5! and 9 ... ♗xf4? 10 ♗b8 h3 11 b8(♕) ♗xb8 12 ♗xb8 would stop the h-pawn.

After 9 ... ♗b8! came **10 ♗e5 ♗a7 11 ♗d4** and now **11 ... b2! 12 ♔c2 ♗b8!**. White is one move short – **13 ♗e5 h3 14 ♗xb8 h2 15 ♗e5 b1(♕)+! 16 ♔xb1 h1(♕)+**.

The winnable hierarchy comes with a few caveats. The biggest is: A winning 'how' matters more. Case in point:

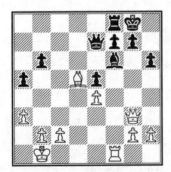

Kobalia – Gershon
Kharkov 2002

White to play

White saw that the only targets were at b6 and f7, and the only immediate threat he could come up with was **1 ♕e3!**. Then 1 ... b5 2 ♕b6 wins material, while 1 ... ♕c7 2 ♖f3, with the idea of ♕f2 and ♖c3 would make some progress.

But what if Black meets a forcing move with a forcing move? After **1 ... ♕c5**, White knew that trading queens was dubious, particularly if he also traded rooks. Bishops of opposite color endgames are at the bottom of the hierarchy and are hard to win even when two or three pawns ahead.

But White can ask himself the obvious question: If I did play **2 ♕xc5 bxc5**, how could I win?

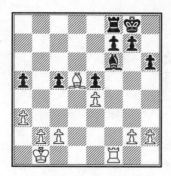

White to play

The answer is: "My king and rook can go after the targets at a5 and c5." That's why White sought this ending and why it turned out to be so easily won. He played **3 ♖f3** and Black stopped the threat of ♖b3-b5 with **3 ... ♖b8**.

White has a simple winning plan beginning with trading rooks, **4 ♔a2! ♔f8 5 ♖b3!**. Now 5 ... ♖c8 6 ♖b7 ♗e7 7 ♔b3 would leave Black paralyzed.

Instead he played **5 ... ♖xb3 6 ♔xb3**. You should be able to see that White's king must win either the a-or c-pawns.

But there is still a finesse to two to appreciate, Play continued **6 ... ♗g5 7 ♔a4 ♗d2 8 ♔b5 ♔e7**.

White to play

Once again White has a choice. But it's an easier choice if he asks himself one more time: How can I win?

The answer is: "With a passed a-pawn." Black would have to give up his bishop to stop it.

So instead of 9 ♔xc5? ♗c1!, White played **9 a4!** with the idea of 10 c3 and 11 ♔xa5.

Black found nothing better than **9 ... ♗c1** and the outcome was clear after **10 ♔xa5! ♗xb2 11 c4! f5 12 ♔b6 ♗c3 13 a5 ♗xc5+ 14 ♔xa5**.

And if you're wondering why White spent a tempo on 11 c4!, the answer is that it stops Black from getting his bishop onto the a7-g1 diagonal. White may be able to find another winning plan after 11 ♔b5 c4 12 ♗xc4 ♗d4! 13 a5 ♔d6. But it's not worth investigating when you already have one.

By playing over master games you can often find the *enough* moment. It may be the point when the player with advantage traded queens and gave up the initiative. It may be when he took an irrevocable step that led to a winning heavy-piece endgame. It may be when he created a material imbalance that was accompanied by a big positional plus. These are the moments worth studying when it comes to winnability.

And once again, some quiz positions:

Quiz

32
Bagirov – Mikhalchishin
Moscow 1981

Black to play

Does Black have realistic winning chances?

33
Pinter – Timman
Las Palmas 1982

Black to play

Same question: Does Black have realistic winning chances?

34
Bareev – Fominyk
Sochi 2004

White to play

Where do White's winning chances lie? What specific steps can he take?

35
Gelfand – Svidler
Moscow 2006

White to play

White has an extra pawn but Black's last move, ... ♖b8, creates problems. How should he proceed?

36
M. Gurevich – Adorjan
Akureyri 1988

White to play

What move should White consider first? And does it work?

White to play

How should White proceed?

Chapter Seven:
Easier

You read game notes all the time that say Black 'has a difficult position'. This sounds like the annotator is saying 'Black is worse'. Or perhaps he means 'Black is much worse'. Or even 'Black may be completely lost but my computer can't find a forced win for White'.

He could mean any of those. But experienced players know that 'difficult' can be taken literally.

Some positions are simply harder to play than others: It is more difficult to find the best move, or even a good move, in them.

Other positions are relatively easy to play. That makes them more attractive to a master, even though a computer may evaluate them as slightly inferior to the difficult alternatives.

The machine must be objective. But you're not a machine and you're allowed to be subjective when it means being pragmatic. Masters steer their way into 'easier' positions all the time.

Even the strongest masters do. After 15 moves of a Scotch Game at Nanjing 2009, Magnus Carlsen had given up a pawn but had two bishops and more space than his opponent, Peter Leko. Carlsen conceded afterwards that he had no advantage. But "it is much easier to play," he said, and that was enough for him. He won.

Here's an illustration of how 'easier' works.

Bartel – Krasenkow
Polish Championship,
Warsaw 2010

Black to play

Black is a pawn down and faced with the prospect of losing another, on d7. If he defends it with 1 ... ♖ad8 or 1 ... ♖fd8, White plays 2 h5. After the Black knight retreats to f8 or h8, White makes inroads with 3 ♘h4 and 4 ♘g6. That would sentence Black to difficult defense with virtually no counterplay.

He made a practical decision. He chose **1 ... ♗c5** to get the most piece activity he could. Then 2 ♕xd7 ♕xe4? doesn't work (3 ♕e6+ ♔h7 4 ♖h5 mate or 3 ... ♖f7 4 ♕xf7+! ♔xf7 5 ♘g5+).

But 2 ... ♕xd7 3 ♖xd7 ♘e7 4 ♖h5 ♖ad8 or 4 ... g6 5 ♘xe5 gxh5 can make White's life difficult.

After 1 ... ♗c5! it was White's turn to weigh his future. He can avoid the complications with **2 ♘e1** and then **2 ... ♘e7 3 ♖f3**, so that his rook escapes. Then after the natural **3 ... d6** and **4 ♕e2**:

White to play

But he still has some difficult choices to make as he tries to unravel his forces, such as with 5 ♖fd3, followed by 6 ♔h2, 7 f3 and ♘c2-e3.

In the end White rejected both the 2 ♕xd7 ending and the 2 ♘e1 regrouping. He chose **2 h5!** even though it traps his rook after 2 ... ♘e7.

"Of course, computers condemn the Exchange sacrifice," he wrote. "But after it, White's play is very simple." On the other hand, he added, "Black's defense, in view of his weakness and his useless bishop on c5, is very hard."

What White meant is that after **3 ♘h4 ♘xf5 4 ♘xf5** he can just throw everything he has against the target at g7.

Black to play

What's more, his moves are easy to find. He can't be stopped from getting his queen and rook to the g-file. He can also use his bishop to attack f6 from h4 and look for a chance to break through at g7.

This kind of pragmatism separates many of today's masters from the maximalists of the past. Great players like Alexander Alekhine or Mikhail Botvinnik claimed they always sought the objectively best move. It didn't matter how difficult it was to wade through the complications. They wanted the best.

Today's masters are willing to admit when they take the easy way out – and they say there's nothing wrong with it. They still want more out of a position than non-masters. But they recognize the limits of what you can do while your clock is burning minutes.

In this game, White created a situation in which he can play his next five or so moves almost with his eyes closed. Play proceeded with **4 ... d6 5 ♕f3 ♕f7 6 ♕g4 ♔h7 7 ♖d3 ♖h8 8 ♗h4 ♔g8 9 ♖g3 ♖h7**. White was ready to open his eyes and look for big tactics.

White to play

White found **10 ♕f3!**, which threatens 11 ♖xg7+! ♖xg7 12 ♘h6+ and 13 ♘xf7. If Black stops that, White has a second idea, less explosive but effective just the same. He can play 11 ♖g6 followed by 12 ♕g4 and 13 h6, which must win in the long run.

Don't think that White saw all that when he sacrificed the Exchange. But he didn't need to. He saw the positional compensation. We'll expand on that in the next chapter.

But for the moment, let's appreciate how much White benefited from pragmatism. The bonus he got from 2 h5 and 4 ♘xf5 was being able to play several 'easier' moves that were obviously good. Black, with a much broader choice of moves of uncertain value, had a tougher task.

Work Load

Let's put that into perspective: Most would-be-masters can make the first ten or so moves of a game without thinking. They rely on opening theory they memorized.

A typical game lasts another 20 to 30 moves beyond that. Now, suppose we subtract the automatic moves, such as recaptures and responses to simple threats and checks from those 20 to 30 moves. What's left?

The bottom line is you may face no more than 10 to 15 somewhat hard choices in a game. Those choices typically cost you two thirds to three quarters of the clock time you spend on the entire game.

Being able to play five 'easier' moves, means reducing your work load considerably. This helps explain why you see masters winning tournaments while taking less clock time than their opponents.

Consider how Black reduced his work load to a minimum in this example.

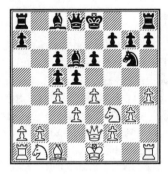

Alekseev – Radjabov
Sochi 2008

Black to play

As in many modern opening positions, the tension in the center is deliberate. White is reluctant to exchange on d5 (say 1 ... 0-0 2 exd5) because that would undouble Black's pawns (2 ... cxd5) and liberate the c8-bishop.

Black, on the other hand, has to think twice about exchanging on c4 or e4 because it would leave him with ugly, apparently undissolvable c-pawns. And 1 ... d4? is a positional error that closes the position to the benefit of White's knights. Therefore you might expect the center to remain the way it is for several more moves.

Nevertheless, once Black saw **1 ... dxc4! 2 dxc4 e5!** he realized how strong it was. How strong – and how practical.

Black can continue with a maneuver of his knight through f8 and e6 to the splendid d4 square. Unlike some good (but impractical) plans, this one cannot be stopped.

Because of White's weakness at f3, once the knight lands on d4 he will be more or less forced into ♘xd4. Then ... cxd4 will turn Black's pawns from a liability into a major asset. He will have a protected passer on d4 and no weak pawns.

White had a lot to think about in the next three turns. Black didn't.

Play continued **3 ♘bd2 ♘f8 4 ♘f1 ♘e6 5 ♘e3 ♘d4 6 ♘xd4 cxd4 7 ♘f5**.

Black to play

Black has his first real choice since 2 ... e5!. He considered preserving his bishop with 7 ... ♗f8 and then driving the knight back with 8 ... g6.

That's not a bad plan. The knight won't find any great squares and Black's bishops look good after, perhaps, 8 h5 g6 9 hxg6 fxg6 10 ♘h6 ♗e6.

Yet Black opted for a simpler policy – largely because it was simpler and easier. He can trade bishops and castle, followed by piling up on the b-file.

It was, once again, a plan that couldn't be forestalled and required hardly any calculation. Play went **7 ... ♗b4+ 8 ♗d2 ♗xd2+ 9 ♕xd2 0-0**.

After **10 g4** Black looked at 10 ... c5 but had doubts about what would happen after 11 ♕g5 because a trade of queens helps White.

Instead, he played **10 ... f6** and there followed **11 f3 ♗e6 12 c5**.

Black to play

Black finds himself with an opportunity to carry out another eyes-closed plan. He can double his heavy pieces against the target at b2 by means of ... a5, ... ♕b8 followed by ... ♖a7-b7 or ... ♕b4/ ... ♖fb8.

The effectiveness of this plan was shown by the next few moves, **12 ... a5 13 b3 ♕b8 14 ♔f2** (not 14 ♘e7+ ♔f7 15 ♘xc6? ♕c7).

Black had more 'easier' moves coming up and his advantage grew with **14 ... ♖a7 15 ♖hc1 ♕b4** in view of 16 ♕xb4 axb4 17 ♖c2 ♖fa8 or, as the game went, with **16 ♕d3 a4!**. He won.

136

Of course, he made some difficult choices in the course of the game, such as 1 ... dxc4 and 10 ... f6 and the rejection of 7 ... ♗f8. But he also played many more 'easier' moves. That's the mark of a pragmatic master.

The 1987 world championship match was a case study of how to shift the work load to your opponent. Of the eight decisive games, six were lost due to time pressure mistakes by the player who had been repeatedly forced to make hard choices earlier.

Anatoly Karpov said it was because of difficult middlegame decisions he had to make in the critical, final game that he didn't have 20 seconds at the point when the game – and match – were decided. "Imagine," he said years later. "For 20 seconds I lost the world championship title, and if you're talking about money, 600,000 dollars."

Here's another key moment in the match.

Kasparov – Karpov
World Championship,
fourth game, 1988

White to play

White spent 34 minutes on this move. But thanks to his decision he didn't spend more than 14 minutes on any of the game's remaining moves.

The press room GMs expected a Kasparovian 1 ♘f5 because it complicates, e.g. 1 ... ♕c5 2 ♘h6+! ♔f8 3 ♖xf6! gxf6 3 ♗d5, with a brutal attack.

Objectively, 1 ♘f5 may be the best move. But it leaves White with a lot to think about after 1 ... ♕d8 or 1 ... ♕e6. Black has a difficult defense but White has a difficult attack.

Instead, White forced matters with **1 ♕e2** and then **1 ... ♘xc1 2 ♖axc1**. Black replied **2 ... d6**.

White to play

Black was nearly half an hour ahead on the clock. But his time edge soon vanished because White could play several progress-making plus-moves, such as ♖f4, ♖cf1, ♕d3 and ♘f5.

Black, on the other hand, has to decide what to do with his center pawns (... c6 or ... c5), to complete development and to watch out for an Exchange sacrifice on f6.

Play went **3 ♖f4 c6 4 ♖cf1** and now he had to avoid 4 ... ♗e6? 5 ♖xf6! gxf6 6 ♗e4 with another strong attack.

He spent time to find **4 ... ♕e5** and then, after **5 ♕d3**, to choose **5 ... ♗d7**, avoiding another strong sacrifice, 5 ... ♕h5? 6 ♖xf6!.

By now White was ready to force a trade of minor pieces, **6 ♘f5 ♗xf5 7 ♖xf5**.

Black to play

Afterwards, analysis determined that Black should have retreated his queen to e7, now or on the next move. But in trying to navigate his way through the complications, he chose **7 ... ♕e6 8 ♕d4 ♖e7?** and there followed **9 ♕h4! ♘d7 10 ♗h3! ♘f8**.

White's advantage had grown and he was ahead on the clock. Once again the GM analysts argued in favor of a sharp candidate, such as 11 ♖xf7 or 11 ♖g5 or even 11 ♖b5.

But White spent just four minutes on the safe – and 'easier' – **11 ♖5f3!**. It forces a highly favorable endgame, **11 ... ♕e5 12 d4 ♕e4 13 ♕xe4 ♖xe4** and then 14 ♖xf7 ♖xe3 15 ♖xb7 would have won quickly. It was a rare case of Karpov being outplayed in a relatively simple position – and it happened because the work load had been shifted to him.

Easiness Equation

Of course, having an easier choice of moves isn't always a good thing. The simplest positions of all to play occur when your king is being checked all over the board. You are forced to play the only legal move available. Your moves are easy to find – but you're about to be checkmated.

On the other hand:

White to play

White has a huge choice. There are at least 18 good moves. Databases say 1 ♗h3 is best. But the 17 others are nearly as good.

Over the next several moves, White will continue to have more than a dozen more or less equal moves. Finding the best one is difficult. But only when White is close to mate will finding the best move matter much. Bottom line: The difficulty factor isn't in the slightest way significant in some positions.

Taking the 'easier' option makes its biggest impact when there is more than one good candidate and the theoretically best move, the one endorsed by computers, lies outside a human's comfort zone.

Cao – Almasi
Heviz 2003

Black to play

Black had sacrificed a pawn to obtain his queenside attack. He could cash in with 1 ... c3+, since 2 ♔a3?? allows 2 ... ♖xa5 mate.

But White had been planning to give up his bishop when he had to. He played 2 ♗xc3.

It should be clear that 2 ... dxc3+ 3 ♕xc3 favors Black. A computer would like 2 ... dxc3+. But winning with an extra piece versus three pawns in this position is no simple matter.

Since Black's position seems good enough to win in the middlegame, he should also consider 1 ... cxb3. But 2 ♗xf8 isn't clear after 2 ... ♖xf8 3 ♕b4! or 2 ... bxc2 3 ♗b4.

In the end, Black took the easy way out. He chose **1 ... c3+** and then **2 ♗xc3 ♖c8!**.

White to play

Black prepares to take on c3 under much better circumstances than 2 ... dxc3+. The key tactical point is that if the bishop retreats, Black has ... ♖xc2+!.

One line runs 3 ♗d2 ♖xc2+! and Black wins after 4 ♔xc2 ♕xb3+ 5 ♔c1 ♖c8+. Not much better is 3 ♗b4 ♖xc2+! 4 ♔xc2 ♕xb3+ 5 ♔d2 ♗xb4+.

White recognized how hopeless his position would be in those lines. He played 3 **♗xd4!**.

This is best because if Black wins the queen, 3 ... ♖xc2+ 4 ♔xc2 ♕xb3+ 5 ♔d2 ♗b4+ 5 ♔e3 ♗xe1, White can hold out for quite a while by playing 6 ♖hxe1 exd4+ 7 ♘xd4.

Once again we would have a situation in which Black should win because of superior material, a queen versus a rook and some pawns. But he would have to navigate slowly, perhaps with 7 ... ♕b4 8 ♖eb1 ♕c5 9 ♖xb5 ♕c3, and can't expect to force resignation for many moves.

Black shouldn't have to work that hard. He didn't because he met 3 ♗xd4 with **3 ... exd4!**.

White to play

Black still threatens ... ♖xc2+. But he can also attack with simple moves he doesn't have to calculate, such as ... ♕e5, ... ♖c3 and ... ♗b4 or ... ♕c5/ ... ♖c8.

The only variation he needed to check was 4 ♘xd4 ♕e5, which turns out to be winning (5 ♕e3 ♗c5 6 c3 b4!).

The game went **4 ♕d2 ♕e5 5 b4 ♖c3 6 f4 ♕c7 7 ♕f2** and now 7 ... ♖c8 was

140

the fastest of a number of winning lines. By restraining himself earlier – passing up 2 ... dxc3+ and then 3 ... ♖xc2+ – he saved time and energy.

'Easier' also helps guide masters in the endgame. This leads them to make choices that seems at odds with material.

Belikov – Saulin
Russian Championship
1995

White to play

Black has just moved a ♘ to d7 to deter ♘b6 or ♗b6. But he failed to notice that **1 ♗b6!** is still possible because after **1 ... ♘xb6 2 ♘b3!** White wins material.

Black's queen isn't trapped. But if it escapes to a4, he allows 3 ♘xb6, forking three heavy pieces and winning the Exchange.

Black made a savvy judgment. Rather than 2 ... ♕a4 he played **2 ... ♘xd5!** and then **3 ♘xa5 ♘c3!**.

Instead of being the Exchange down he preferred to give up a lot more material, a queen for two minor pieces. What was he thinking?

He was thinking that both material deficits – down the Exchange or giving up the queen for two pieces – are enough to lose. But there's a practical difference.

White to play

His opponent would have an elementary task of winning with the extra Exchange in the 2 ... ♕a4 3 ♘xb6 line. Routine moves would do the trick.

But winning wouldn't be routine in the diagram after 4 bxc3 ♘xa5. White's material advantage is much greater but Black has excellent positional trumps such as the targets at c3 and c4. White should win but the process requires a lot more thinking.

White understood this just as Black did, and that's why he chose **4 ♘xc6!** instead of 4 bxc3. This leads to a forcing variation, **4 ... ♘xd1 5 ♘xe7+ ♔f8 6 ♘xc8.**

Black to play

Now White is the Exchange and a pawn ahead and would have another easy time clinching the point after, say, 6 ... ♖xc8 7 ♖fxd1.

For example, 7 ... ♗xc4 8 ♖ac1! or 7 ... ♗xb2 8 ♖ab1 ♗e5 9 ♖xb7. No better is 7 ... ♔e7 because of 8 ♖ab1 ♗xc4 9 ♖dc1 ♗e6 10 ♖xc8 ♗xc8 11 ♗g4!.

Black cut his material deficit by playing **6 ... ♘xb2** instead of 6 ... ♖xc8. But after **7 ♘b6 ♖a7 8 ♖ab1** his task is fairly simple and Black decided to end matters with **8 ... a5 9 ♖fc1 ♗d4 10 ♖c2 resigns**. Had White chosen 4 bxc3 he'd be playing for at least 10 more moves than he did in the game and some of his decisions would be difficult.

Reducing Three Results to Two

Another cliché that annotators love is: 'Three results are possible'. This is their way of saying the position in question is so double-edged that either player could win, or the game could end up as a draw.

Alternatively, a player will say he avoided a particular line of play because only two results were possible – and that's not good.

Anand – Morozevich
Dortmund 2001

Black to play

Black said he considered 1 ... dxc4 for a long time, with the likely continuation of 2 ♗xc4 b5 3 ♗d3 c5.

But he rejected it because it would probably lead to a middlegame "where only two results were possible."

In other words, he was afraid that if he liquidated tension, only White would have winning chances thanks to greater space and the two bishops. The best Black could hope for then is a draw, he felt. (He left the center tension intact with 1 ... ♗e7 and the third result occurred: He won.)

Increasing the number of possible results is a stock in trade of masters when they are Black and playing a weaker player. To appreciate what's involved, play through grandmaster games, such as by Morozevich when he has Black. Or just look at how masters handle Black in the second or third round of a large Swiss tournament, when they are paired against a lower-rated but not easily beatable opponent. They manage to maximize winning chances while minimizing the chances of the third result, a loss.

There's another skill to be learned: Reducing the number of results from three to two, a draw and a win. This can often be done in a way that also makes your future decisions easier.

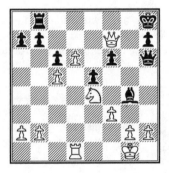

Spassky – Czerniak
Goteborg 1971

Black to play

After Black played **1 ... ♖f8**, White had a lot to consider. He could have invested time in checking out queen moves such as 2 ♕xb7. But he needs to calculate them because Black has prospects such as 2 ... ♕e3+ and 2 ... ♗xf3 3 gxf3 ♖g8+ or 3 ... ♕e3+. It's conceivable that White could even get mated if he overlooks a shot.

But why calculate when there is an alternative like **2 ♕xf8+! ♕xf8 3 fxg4** ?

White doesn't have to see far at all to play this with confidence. He might notice that 4 d7 looks strong. He might also see that if 4 d7 doesn't win quickly, he has a good alternative in 4 ♖f1 followed by a capture on f6. That should win in the long run.

In any case, there is virtually no chance of Black winning. Only two results are possible.

Black to play

Black replied **3 ... ♕d8** and then came **4 d7 ♔g8.** No better was 4 ... ♔g7 5 ♘d6 ♕xd7 6 ♘f5+.

The game ended with **5 ♘xf6+! ♔f7 6 ♘e4 ♔e7 7 ♘d6,** when **Black resigned** in view of 8 ♘xb7 (or 7 ... ♕xd7 8 ♘f5+).

Of course, Boris Spassky could calculate well enough to check out all the variations after 3 fxg4 until they reached a 'and White wins' end. But often there are simply too many lines that last too many moves into the future to count out and evaluate.

Reducing the number of results becomes more important as the inability to calculate with certainty increases. Consider the next diagram. White has temporarily sacrificed a pawn and clearly intends to take on c6. But how should he capture?

Dominguez – Tiviakov
Wijk aan Zee 2010

White to play

Sure, 1 ♗xc6 looks like it must be best because it forks the rooks. The likely continuations are 1 ... ♗xh3 and 1 ... ♗b7 and White will win the Exchange.

There is no quick forced win then. That is, there is no sequence of White shots that will bring Black to his knees in a reasonably short number of moves. Moreover, there is no way to force a trade of queens

White would have to be careful not to allow Black's queen to threaten mate on the c6-h1 diagonal. Yes, White *should* win. But he *could* lose.

The alternative is **1 ♕xc6**. Then White can force a position that has only two possible outcomes, and the winning chances are vastly greater than the drawing chances. For example 1 ... ♗e6 2 ♕b5! and Black is quite lost (2 ... ♕xb5 3 axb5 or 2 ... ♕e7 3 ♗xa8 ♖xa8 4 ♕xa5).

In the game, Black chose the superior **1 ... ♗f5** and he met **2 ♕b5** with **2 ... ♗e4**.

White to play

But now comes **3 ♖c4!**, forcing a liquidation into an easily won endgame. Black must reply **3 ... ♕xb5 4 axb5 ♗xg2 5 ♔xg2**.

Black's knight becomes useless after **5 ... ♘b4**. The White rooks and b-pawn will decide after **6 b6 ♖e7 7 ♖c7!** or, as the game went, with **6 ... ♖ab8 7 ♖d7 h6 8 b7** followed by ♗a7 or ♗f4.

Reducing the number of outcomes from three to two only works if there is a very good chance of a win. In the last example, 1 ♕xc6! would have been 1 ♕xc6? if Black had strong drawing chances. Then 1 ♗xc6 would have been superior, despite the complications.

Masters are also good at reducing three results to two when on the defensive. Here's an example.

Sax – Ehlvest
Rotterdam 1989

Black to play

White has just shifted his rook to g3. If Black replies 1 ... cxd4? White has 2 ♗xh7+! ♘xh7 3 ♘gxf7, forking heavy pieces and also threatening 4 ♘h6+ and 5 ♘g6 mate.

Black can't stop that with 1 ... h6 (2 ♗h7+!) and he saw that 1 ... ♕xd4 2 ♗xh7+ costs the queen.

145

That seems to indicate 1 ... g6 is best. But playing the pawn move requires analyzing variations such as 2 ♘xh7, with lines such as 2 ... ♔xh7 3 dxc5 bxc5 4 ♗xg6+ or 3 ... ♕xc5 4 ♘xg6 or 3 ... ♕c7 4 cxb6 axb6 5 h5! ♘xh5 6 ♖h1. Black may be OK in one of those lines but it takes an effort to be sure.

Black took the practical way out. He chose **1 ... ♕xd4!** after all, because **2 ♗xh7+ ♘xh7 3 ♖xd4 ♖xd4** kills the attack at a small material cost. Play went **4 ♕e3 ♘xg5 5 hxg5**.

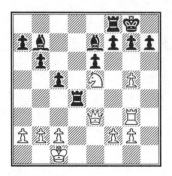

Black to play

It may not be obvious but White's attacking chances are extinguished. An added benefit is that Black's moves are easier to find. After **5 ... ♖e4 6 ♕c3 ♗d6** the kingside pawns became targets.

White was losing after **7 f4 ♖xf4 8 ♖d3 ♗d5 9 ♘f3 ♖g4! 10 ♕e1 c4 11 ♖d4 ♖xg2**.

'Taking the easy way out' used to be considered laziness. Masters know that moves like 1 ... ♕xd4! save energy but also half points. And with that it's time again for you to work on some quiz positions.

Quiz

38

Shirov – Ivanchuk
Buenos Aires 1994

Black to play

Black has all the winning chances. But White has real drawing chances. What should Black play?

39
Spraggett – Yusupov
Candidates match 1989

White to play

How can White make his life easier?

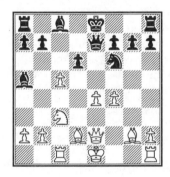

40
Novik – Dvoiris
Moscow 1992

Black to play

White has just played 1 c5! so that 1 ... dxc5 2 e5 followed by ♘d5 after the knight retreats. Should Black avoid that? And, if so, how?

41
J. Polgar – Leko
Dortmund 1996

Black to play

Black should be OK if he retreats his attacked bishop to c6. What else is there to consider?

Chapter Eight:
Comp

A master's superiority in evaluating a position is most pronounced when it comes to that vague term compensation. He knows 'comp' when he sees it.

When considering a sacrifice a master might look just two moves into the future. That's when he can conclude that he would receive worthwhile goodies in return for the material he's giving up. "This must be sound," he may say to himself. He can stop calculating there.

The non-master can't. He typically has doubts about whether the sacrifice is worthwhile, less than worthwhile – or a blunder that will cost him the game. He feels he has to look further, maybe four, five moves or more into the future, hoping to find confirmation of the sack's soundness. Consider this example:

**Kasimdzhanov –
Alekseev**
Elista 2008

Black to play

White has just played a book move, 1 d5. It's another example of little tactics. Black cannot play 1 ... ♘xd5? because 2 ♗xd5 ♖xd5 3 e4 costs a piece.

In previous games, Black retreated, 1 ... ♘e7. Then White gained more space with 2 c4! followed by 3 ♘d2 and 4 e4, and was slightly better. Once again little tactics was the means towards a positional end and edge.

But not in this game. This time Black replied **1 ... ♖xd5 and 2 ♗xd5 ♘xd5**. The players who examined the game afterward fell roughly into two groups:

The first group consisted of amateurs. They wondered what Black was doing. He only gets a pawn for the Exchange. Where is the compensation?

In the second group were masters. They wondered "Why in the world hadn't anyone played 1 ... ♖xd5! before?" Masters saw that Black gains several positional plusses. He ends up with the better center, potential domination of light squares and a good-♘-vs.-bad-♗ matchup. All this comes at a slim material cost.

After **3 ♖fd1 ♞b6** Black hinted that he wanted to dominate the White bishop and rooks with ... ♞a4 followed by ... c4 and ... ♝d3.

White avoided that with **4 a4 a6 5 c4**, freeing his bishop. Black responded by securing a nice outpost at b4 with **5 ... a5!**.

White to play

Only now does Black's compensation appear on the board. He is preparing ... ♞b4 followed by ... ♝c2xa4 or ... ♝d7xa4.

Assessing compensation is often as much as 90 percent evaluation and only 10 percent calculation. A master wouldn't have to calculate this far when looking at 1 ... ♖xd5. In fact, all he might have to calculate is seeing that 2 ♝xd5 ♞xd5 3 e4 can be met by 3 ... ♞f4.

In the game White prepared to trade off a Black's knight with **6 ♝c3** and then **6 ... f6 7 ♞d2 ♞b4 8 ♝xb4 cxb4**. This gave Black additional positional plusses: a protected passed pawn and a new target, the c-pawn. White was losing soon after **9 ♖dc1 ♖d8 10 c5 ♝d3 11 ♕e1 ♞d5 12 ♞b3 h6 13 ♖a2 e4** and ... ♞c3.

Compensation is hard to appreciate because, by definition, it is imprecise. If it were precise – if you could look at a knight sacrifice X moves into the future and say "White wins" – it's not a sacrifice with compensation.

That's a combination, without risk. The sacrifice isn't 'real', in Rudolf Spielmann's simple but useful term. Here's a 'sham' sacrifice.

Hulak – Cebalo
Zagreb 1982

Black to play

Black obtained a positional edge with **1 ... ♖xc3!**. The capture has been carried out in thousands of similar Sicilian Defenses. Sometimes it's a sound sacrifice. Sometimes it's unsound.

But this isn't a real sacrifice. After **2 bxc3 ♘a2** Black must regain the Exchange (3 ♖b1? ♘xc3).

After the game continuation, **3 ♕d3 ♘xc1 4 ♖xc1**, material is equal. Black has simply carried out an indirect trade of a pair of rooks and knights

He did it for a positional purpose, to obtain the superior pawn structure. In other words, this is a *petite combinaison*. Black won eventually by a preponderance of positional edges.

In contrast, here is perhaps the first example of a real ... ♖xc3 sacrifice in the Sicilian Defense. It was played in a simultaneous exhibition.

Schultz – Alekhine
Stockholm 1914

Black to play

This could have been labeled a combination if the only reply to **1 ... ♖xc3!** were 2 ♕xc3?. Then 2 ... ♘d5! would win material, because of the threats to the queen and the bishop at e3.

Instead, the availability of **2 bxc3** made it a sacrifice. After **2 ... ♘xe4 3 ♕d3 ♘xe3 4 ♕xe3 ♘xc3** material was not equal.

Black had ample comp for the Exchange: two pawns, the two-bishop advantage, and targets to hit at a2 and c2. But this is far from a forced win or a positionally won game.

In fact, when a master spots a promising sacrifice he may not even try to see if there's a forced win. All he needs to know is that the move is worth playing, that there is enough comp.

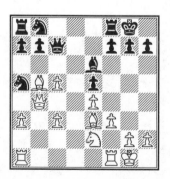

Anand – Wang
Wijk aan Zee 2011

White to play

Vishy Anand had analyzed this late opening position three years before when preparing for a world championship match. But he hadn't gotten a chance to use his analysis until this game because no one had played Black's last move, ... ♗e6, against him.

He finally got his chance to play **1 ♘d4!** in this game. What he remembered from his 2008 analysis was that after **1 ... exd4 2 cxd4** White will have two strong pawns for the knight and the pawns will severely restrict Black's pieces, including the off-side knight at a5. That's more than enough compensation, he concluded.

His evaluation turned out to be exactly right when play continued **2 ... ♘bc6 3 ♕c3 ♘e7 4 ♖fd1 ♖ad8 5 ♗f2 a6 6 ♗g3 ♕c8 7 ♗f1**.

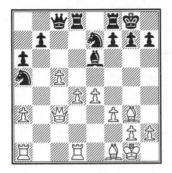

Black to play

White hadn't calculated this far previously and didn't know, for example, how good 7 ... ♘ac6 8 ♗d6! would be. It wasn't necessary to do that as long as 1 ♘d4 passed the 'sufficient comp' test.

The game went **7 ... b6 8 ♖ab1! ♘b3 9 ♖xb3 ♗xb3 10 ♕xb3 bxc5 11 d5!** and the bishops and pawns led to an easy win, in view of ♕b6 followed by ♗xa6 or ♗d6.

Alexander Alekhine underlined this ability – to conclude 'it must be sound!' – when he explained why he gave up the Exchange in an endgame at Nottingham 1936. "One of the combinations that an experienced player does not need to calculate to the finish. He *knows* that under given circumstances the king's side pawns must become overwhelming," Alekhine wrote.

Of course, many players are suspicious of appearances. They'll want to calculate further. How much further is a personal matter.

Ljubojevic – Portisch
Lucerne 1982

White to play

One of the first things you should notice is that f7 is unprotected. That makes it a potential target.

The second thing to notice is that f7 can be attacked by 1 ♗c4, which is also a good positional move. White doesn't expect to win the f-pawn. But he expects that if he gets to play ♗d5 he will have established d5 as a strong outpost.

The third thing a master would notice is that the bishop is unprotected on c4 and that 1 ♗c4 would allow 1 ... ♘xe4. Then 2 ... ♕xc4 as well as discovered attacks on White's queen, such as 2 ... ♘xg3, are threatened.

Nevertheless, White played **1 ♗c4** and then **1 ... ♘xe4 2 ♗d5!**. He might have stopped here and concluded he would have good compensation in view of his control of d5 and the weakness of Black's king position after the inevitable trade of bishops.

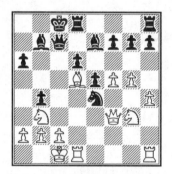

Black to play

But White, perhaps the best calculator of his generation, looked further and saw that 2 ... ♘c5 would not provide Black with adequate king protection because White can play 3 ♘e4!.

His move makes no threat but is just another good 'plus-move', like ♔b1, ♖d2 and ♖hd1, which may be coming up.

White likely looked even further and saw that after 2 ... ♘xg3 3 ♕xg3 he will have good compensation as well as threats once he gets his KR into play via e1 and e4. Here again the future of the rooks is a tipoff to who is improving their position more.

The game went **2 ... ♘xg3 3 ♕xg3 ♔b8 4 ♖he1 ♖c8 5 ♕g2**.

Black to play

If he had seen this far, White couldn't be sure how his sacrifice would turn out. All he would know is that he has good pressure. That's what comp for one pawn often amounts to. It's not an assurance of an advantage. It is merely an indication of promising prospects.

The indication turned out to be accurate. After a few routine moves, **5 ... ♗xd5 6 ♖xd5 ♕b6 7 ♖e4!**, Black made one mistake, **7 ... ♖c7?**.

That allowed White to regain his pawn with **8 ♕g4** and ♖xb4 (since 8 ... ♖b7 is met by 9 ♘a5).

It's not the pawn that matters as much as Black's lack of king protection, and the game ended soon after **8 ... ♔a7 9 ♖xb4 ♕e3+ 10 ♔b1 h5? 11 ♕d1 ♖hc8 12 ♕f1**, preparing ♖a5/♖ba4 as well as the immediate 13 ♕xa6+! ♔xa6 14 ♖a5 mate.

Pretty Pictures, Muddier Pictures

Of course, it's possible that White calculated 1 ♗c4 as far as 7 ♖e4 or even further. But, as we said earlier, masters distrust a lot of calculation. They know you can't calculate everything. And if you try, the picture gets muddier, the conclusions you draw are more dubious and the likelihood for error soars dramatically.

The amateur who feels he has to look six or seven moves ahead to justify a sacrifice is deluding himself. A revealing look at how a master thinks was given by David Bronstein in his memoirs.

Palatnik – Bronstein
Tbilisi 1973

Black to play

Bronstein took half an hour before choosing **1 ... ♕h5**, which threatens 2 ... ♗xh3. Play continued **2 g4 ♗xg4**.

The spectators concluded that he had invested his time on 1 ... ♕h5 because he expected 2 g4 and needed to calculate deeply to be sure that the bishop sacrifice was sound.

Wrong. Bronstein revealed that what he was really thinking about in the diagram was what he would do if White replied to 1 ... ♕h5 with 2 h4!. He eventually decided that Black has no advantage and he would have offered a draw.

The reason why he didn't agonize over the consequences of 2 g4 ♗xg4 3 hxg4 ♘xg4 was that the sacrifice is almost a no-brainer, another case of 'it must be good'.

It's true that Black only gets two pawns for his bishop. But he obtains strong threats, beginning with 4 ... ♕h2 mate and the longer-term ... ♖d6-g6. Thanks to visualization, Black saw that White's queen and knight will be in no position to defend the kingside.

White to play

Bronstein's judgment was confirmed when play went **4 ♗f4 ♗d6! 5 ♗xd6 ♖xd6 6 ♖fe1 ♖g6**.

White's defense fell apart after **7 ♘c3 ♕h2+ 8 ♔f1 ♘f6 9 ♗e4 ♕h3+ 10 ♔e2 ♘xe4 11 ♘xe4 ♖e6**.

What allows a master to be confident when he stops calculating? There are several factors, including the number of positional plusses and threats that a sacrifice offers. But often he likes the looks of a future position – literally.

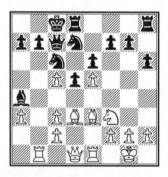

Shirov – Zsuzsa Polgar
Pardubice 1994

White to play

White is a pawn ahead but may lose one of his center pawns after say, 1 ♗d4 g5 and ... g4.

He chose **1 ♖b4**. You can argue about whether this should have been prepared by 1 ♕e2 first. But there is little doubt that White has ample compensation – and a much easier position to play – after the sacrifice. Play went **1 ... ♘xb4 2 axb4**.

What has White gotten for the Exchange? Well, for starters, his vulnerable pawn at c5 is solidly protected and part of an aggressive phalanx that threatens to rip open Black's king protection. In return for the half-open b-file White has the use of a more valuable a-file.

Black to play

White threatens to win with 3 ♕a1 ♗c6 4 b5. But it isn't that threat as much as the purely visual appearance of this position that tells a master that 1 ♖b4! is sound.

This became clearer after Black defended with **2 ... a6**. White would have had good chances after 3 ♕a1. But he wanted to get his knight, not the bishop, to d4.

He saw that **3 ♘d4** ♕xe5 makes 4 ♕a1! strong. When he considered the alternative, 3 ... ♘xe5, he saw 4 ♗f4! was powerful.

And perhaps most important, he realized that if Black replied to 3 ♘d4 with 3 ... ♗c6, eliminating the dangers of ♕a1, White can consolidate with 4 f4!.

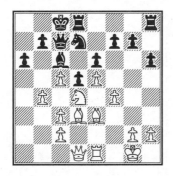

Black to play

Now all of his weak pawns have gone from being targets to strengths. And how does Black stop a winning plan such as ♕a1 and ♖b1 followed by ♘xc6 and/or b4-b5?

Black preferred **3 ... ♘b8** to 3 ... ♗c6. White obtained a wonderful position with routine moves, **4 ♕a1 ♗c6 5 f4 g6 6 ♗f2 ♖hg8 7 ♖b1** and ♗h4-f6, and won.

In fact, his position is so strong after 3 ... ♘b8 that 4 b5! axb5 5 ♗xb5 would crumple Black's position faster.

For example, 5 ... ♗xb5 6 ♘xb5 ♛a5 7 ♛b1 followed by ♛b2 and ♖a1. Or 6 ... ♛xe5 7 ♗d4 ♛g5 8 ♘a7+ and ♛b1 wins.

The flip side to liking the looks of your side of the board is liking the appearance of damage that a sacrifice inflicts on the enemy position.

Akopian – Shirov
Khanty Mansiysk 2007

Black to play

White seems to hold the upper hand, thanks to a slight lead in development, the target pawn at a6 and his outpost at d5. Black proved that judgment was wrong with **1 ... ♗xe3**.

Now 2 dxe3 ♘d4! would favor Black, e.g. 3 ♛xa6? ♘e2+ and 4 ... ♘xc3 or 3 ♛d1 ♘xf3+ 4 ♛xf3 ♗c6, when the targets at c4 and e4 matter more than the one at d6.

Therefore White retook **2 fxe3** so he could meet **2 ... ♘d4** with **3 ♛xa6** and not lose material. The game continued **3 ... ♘e2+ 4 ♔f2 ♘xc3 5 dxc3** and then **5 ... ♔e7!**, the best way of defending the d6-pawn.

White to play

The forcing moves are over and that means it would have been extremely hard for Black to calculate much beyond this position when he decided on 1 ... ♗xe3!. Nevertheless, he could be pretty certain that the sacrifice is sound because of those two sets of doubled White pawns and the other target at a2.

Now that we've reached this position we can look at concrete lines. After 6 ♖d1 Black meets the ♛xd6+ threat with 6 ... ♛c7, creating his own threat, to trap the queen with 7 ... ♖a8.

Then 7 ♕a3 ♖a8 8 ♕c1 ♖a4 followed by 9 ... ♖ha8 and ... ♗c6 or ... ♗e6, for example, grants Black terrific queenside pressure.

White chose **6 ♘d2** instead but Black proved he had adequate compensation after **6 ... ♖a8 7 ♕b7 ♕a5** and 8 ... ♖hb8. He eventually won after **8 ♕b2 ♖hb8 9 ♕c2 ♖xb1 10 ♘xb1 ♖b8 11 ♘d2 ♕a4**.

Compensation 101

Being able to evaluate comp may seem like a gift, like being born with perfect eyesight or perfect pitch. It isn't. It's a matter of training.

The best way to acquire it is by looking at master games and recognizing the sacrifices that worked and the ones that didn't. We're talking about 'real' sacrifices, in Spielmann's term, not combinations. Your goal is to develop a feeling for the individual factors that make a sacrifice sound.

You can compose a list. In *Rethinking the Chess Pieces*, I identified five criteria that are useful in evaluating an Exchange sacrifice. For example, such a sacrifice can be sound 'when the rooks can't behave like rooks'.

In other words, it makes sense to give up a rook for a minor piece when your opponent's rooks are restricted by the pawn structure. Then his material advantage is negated, and what matters is the positional plusses you got in return. "None of my rooks did anything," Sam Shankland complained after fellow GM Alexander Shabalov sacrificed an Exchange against him in the 2011 U.S. Championship and won easily.

Another criterion in a sound Exchange sacrifice is the presence of several minor pieces on the board. Black's sacrifice in the following game wouldn't be sound if he didn't have two knights.

Baburin – Mik. Tseitlin
Cappelle la Grande 1994

Black to play

Black has a target at c4 and possibly g4. A natural way to proceed is 1 ... ♖b4 followed by ... ♕b6 to try to loosen White's defense of the c-pawn. Black seems to be making progress after 2 ♖ac1 ♕b6. Or he could try to find a way to make ... h5 work.

But he preferred **1 ... ♖xb2!** ("Naturally!" he said afterwards) **2 ♕xb2 ♘xc4**. What made the sacrifice natural to him was that because he had two knights compared with White's one knight, he could be assured of occcupying the powerful outpost at e5. That's by far the biggest positional asset in the position.

Play continued **3 ♕c3 ♘fe5**.

White to play

This could be an example of a sacrifice decision that was 90 percent evaluation. All that Black had to see when he chose 1 ... ♖xb2 was he would get an unopposed knight on e5 after 4 ♘xe5 ♘xe5. Further, he could visualize that ... h5 is more dangerous than in the previous diagram.

If White doesn't initiate a trade on e5, Black will play, ... ♘xf3+ followed by ... ♘e5. It doesn't take Kasparovian calculation to see that if White allows ... f3, his king position is on the point of collapse.

White tried to defend against ... h5 with **4 ♘h2 h5 5 ♖fe1 hxg4 6 hxg4**. But after **6 ... ♕g5!** he was clearly worse. Defending the g4-pawn with 7 ♗f3 ♘xf3+ or 7 ♗h3 f3! and ... ♕h4 will turn out disastrously.

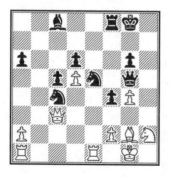

White to play

White realized that his best chance was also an Exchange sacrifice, **7 f3! ♘e3 8 ♖xe3! fxe3 9 ♖e1** and ♖xe3. But he was losing after **9 ... ♗d7 10 ♖xe3 ♖b8 11 ♘f1 ♖b4 12 ♖e1 ♕f4 13 ♕e3 ♗b5**.

Any would-be master knows the long list of items that comprise a positional advantage. Besides outposts and superior pawn structures, they include unchallenged control of strong diagonals, the two bishops, a weakened enemy king position, strong passed pawns and so on.

If the amount of material being sacrificed is relatively small, any of those plusses may alone qualify as sufficient comp. Here's a striking case.

Polugayevsky – Gelfand
Reggio Emilia 1991-92

Black to play

White has just exchanged pieces on f6, giving up his dark-squared bishop so that he could play ♘e4. His idea is to exploit the targets, the pawns at d5 and b7. He prepares ♘c5 or ♘xf6+ followed by cxd5.

White has not given up material. But he is relying on his sense of compensation: His kingside pawns would be wrecked after 1 ... ♗xh4 2 gxh4. But he feels it would be worthwhile because he would threaten 3 ♘g5 as well as 3 cxd5 ♗xd5 4 ♖xd5! ♕xd5 5 ♘f6+ and ♗xd5.

However, let's turn the board around and think about the position from Black's point of view. What are the positional plusses for him?

Believe it or not, one of the biggest is that pawn at a3. Beginners tend to overrate the value of an advanced pawn simply because it's advanced. Better-than-average players know better than that. But they tend to *undervalue* an advanced blocked pawn simply because it's blocked.

Thanks to a bit of visualization, Black appreciated its true value and played **1 ... dxe4!** and then **2 ♖xd8 ♖fxd8**.

White to play

What matters most is that Black will almost certainly win the pawn at a2, clearing the way for his own a-pawn to queen. For example, 3 ♗xe4 ♘b4 4 ♕b1 ♖d2 followed by, say, ... ♘xa2-c3 and ... a2.

Instead, White tried **3 ♕xe4 ♖d2**. He recognized how lost 4 ♕b1 ♖b2 and ... ♘b4 or even 4 ... ♖xe2 would be.

So he went for broke on the kingside with **4 f4 ♖xa2 5 f5 gxf5 6 ♘xf5**. But after Black forced a trade of rooks with **6 ... ♖a1!** there was nothing to stop his pawn and White lost after a tactical gamble, **7 ♘xe7+ ♘xe7 8 ♖xa1 ♗xa1 9 ♕xb7 ♗d4+ 10 e3 ♗xe3+ 11 ♔f1 ♖a7**.

Threats and Comp

Sophisticated, sound sacrifices require more than just positional plusses. They usually demand threats as well. In the last example Black's a3-pawn meant nothing without Black's threats to win White's a2-pawn. Once Black took on a2, the Black pawn accounted for virtually all of his compensation and it was enough to win.

It's hard to generalize about when the comp you need is primarily positional, when it is mostly material and when it is chiefly a matter of threats. But pawn sacrifices can teach us something. There is no material comp when you give up one pawn, so threats and positional plusses are all that matter.

To deepen your appreciation of compensation, you should look at master games with one-pawn sacks. Avoid mating attack games and focus instead on positional battles, like the following.

Mikhalchishin – Lukin
Moscow 1979

White to play

White can obtain a small edge with the quiet 1 ♘de4. After 1 ... ♘xe4 2 ♘xe4 he is ready to play 3 b3 and 4 ♗e3 or 4 ♗b2 with advantage.

But 2 ... ♖d8 3 b3 d5!? could be messy. White can settle instead for a more secure superiority by means of 3 ♕c2 and 4 ♗e3.

However, White has reason to expect more out of this position than a plus-over-equals edge. He needs the help of little tactics. That directs his attention to a threatening move, 1 ♘a4. But what's the follow-up?

The answer would have to be the positionally desirable 2 c5. That makes both b6 and d6 into very vulnerable – and occupyable – holes.

But there is a risk if Black answers 1 ♘a4 with **1 ... ♕a5** because then **2 c5** puts a pawn hanging.

Black to play

When considering this position, White can more or less rule out all Black replies other than 2 ... ♗xc5. White would simply have a too big an edge at no cost after 2 ... ♖d8? 3 ♘c4.

Therefore, White had to weigh **2 ... ♗xc5** and **3 ♘c4 ♕b5**. Does he have compensation then?

White felt there was enough in **4 b3!**. He threatens 5 ♘xc5 ♕xc5 6 ♗a3, winning the Exchange.

If Black retreats the bishop to e7, he allows 5 ♘ab6 ♖b8 6 ♗f4, and White regains his pawn with interest.

Black might try 4 ... d5 with the idea of 5 ♘xc5 dxc4!. But this fails to 5 ♘c3! ♕b4 6 a3! ♕xc3 7 ♗b2, trapping the queen.

That leaves a retreat along the other diagonal, **4 ... ♗a7** and **5 ♗a3 ♖d8 6 ♖c1**.

Black to play

White could have played differently in the last few moves, such as with 6 ♘d6, and still have plenty of compensation. But the more accurate 6 ♖c1! creates more threats, such as 7 ♗xc6 and then 7 ... ♕xc6 8 ♘cb6 or 7 ... bxc6 8 ♗e7 ♖e8? 9 ♘d6. White won without much difficulty.

A two-pawn sacrifice, not surprisingly, is harder to appraise than a one-pawn offer. But there are some clues. The more pawns that you give up, the greater the role that specific threats play in confirming compensation.

Lautier – Zhukova
Odessa 2006

White to play

What a master notices first when he looks at this position is Black's porous kingside. But he also sees that Black is about to trim down White's attack force with ... ♗f5xd3. That suggests White should consider an f4-f5 sacrifice.

But 1 f5 ♘xf5 has no follow-up move of significance. A master can stop there and dismiss 1 f5?.

White was loyal to the idea of f4-f5. It works so often in similar positions that a master wouldn't walk away from it here.

What if White has greater control of f5? So, a master tries to figure out how to get his knight to d4. He sees **1 b4** with the idea of **1 ... cxb4 2 axb4 ♗xb4** and now **3 ♘d4**.

When you visualize that position:

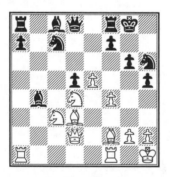

Black to play

You can see that in addition to the now-stronger 4 f5 White has the possibility of 4 ♘c6. The knight fork wouldn't win material by force because Black can reply 4 ... ♗xc3. However, White has more obvious compensation after 5 ♕xc3 – control of dark squares, two bishops. Moreover, he can also regain his pawn immediately by taking on a7 as soon as Black moves his attacked queen.

A master would conclude that Black has to spend a tempo to anticipate 4 ♘c6, say with **3 ... ♗d7**.

This means White has a better chance to push the f-pawn. But **4 f5** will sacrifice a second pawn, 4 ... ♘xf5 5 ♗xf5 and then 5 ... ♗xf5 6 ♘xf5 gxf5.

Black's kingside is broken up but is it worth two pawns? White concluded it was when he saw 7 ♗d4!. That opens up the f-file and protects the knight at c3.

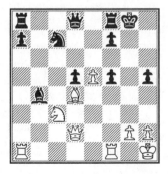

Black to play

White threatens to regain one of his pawns with ♖xf5. But the greater threat is ♕h6 followed by a rook-lift to the g-file (♖xf5-g5+ or ♖f3-g3+).

A master would conclude that the sacrifices have been worthwhile, even without looking at, say, 7 ... ♕d7? 8 ♕g5+, or 7 ... ♘e6 8 ♖xf5 or 7 ... ♔h7 8 ♖xf5.

It was correctly evaluating this position and the one in the previous diagram that played the biggest role in winning this game. In fact, this position never occurred because Black backed out of 4 ... ♘xf5 and chose the inferior 4 ... ♘g4? to eliminate the dark-square bishop.

There followed 5 ♗g3 ♔g7 6 h3!. Now 6 ... ♘h6 loses to 7 e6! (7 ... fxe6 8 ♗e5+ ♔h7 9 fxg6+ ♔g8 10 ♕xh6).

So Black tried 6 ... ♘e3 and the game went 7 ♕xe3 ♗xc3 8 ♖ac1 ♗xd4 9 ♕xd4.

Black to play

Amateurs are often amazed when a position like this comes about. "Did White see this position when he played 4 f5? When he played 1 b4?"

No, of course not. What was crucial is that he saw the compensation in the first pawn sacrifice and the possibility of f4-f5 after 3 ♘d4.

This position in the diagram is won, thanks to threats such as 10 e6+, followed by 11 exd7 or 11 ♗xc7 as well as 10 ♗h4 followed by 11 ♗xd8 or 11 ♗f6+.

In fact, the game ended with **9 ... ♔h7 10 e6! ♘xe6** (10 ... fxe6 11 ♗xc7) **11 fxe6 ♗xe6 12 ♖f6! ♖c8 13 ♖cf1 ♕e7 14 ♕e5 resigns**, in view of threats such as 16 ♕xh5+.

This is the kind of game worth your time. There are a lot more. Thanks to computers it's much easier today to get quick access to hundreds of sacrifices for your training. Pawn sacks, double-pawn sacks, and so on.

You can examine piece sacrifices in general or look specifically at, for example, games with a knight sack on e6 or d5 in a Sicilian Defense. Or when White gives up a bishop or knight on b5, again in a Sicilian. And, of course, there is Black's ... ♖xc3 sacrifice in the Sicilian, perhaps the most common and copied offer of the Exchange in modern chess. There's a mountain of study material out there for the would-be master.

Counter-Sacrifice

It's not just the sacrificer who must understand compensation. It's his opponent as well. Often an opponent can seize the opportunity to counter-sacrifice provided he gets enough of his own compensation.

Let's examine a game with sacrificial offers back and forth. But we'll start with the bare game score. Play these moves over before going on.

Topalov – Gulko, Dos Hermanas 1994: **1 e4 e6 2 d4 d5 3 ♘c3 ♗b4 4 e5 c5 5 a3 ♗xc3+ 6 bxc3 ♘e7 7 ♘f3 b6 8 ♗b5+ ♗d7 9 ♗d3 ♗a4 10 h4 h6 11 h5 ♕c7 12 0-0 ♘d7 13 ♖e1 ♕c6 14 ♖b1 a6 15 ♘d2 cxd4 16 cxd4 ♗b5 17 ♖xb5 axb5 18 ♕e2 ♖a4 19 ♘b3 ♖c4 20 ♗d2 ♘f5 21 ♗b4 ♘xd4 22 ♘xd4 ♖xd4 23 ♗xb5 ♕c8 24 ♖d1 ♖xb4 25 axb4 ♕c3 26 ♕g4 ♕xe5 27 c4 f5 28 ♕g6+ ♔e7 29 cxd5 exd5 30 ♗xd7 ♔xd7 31 ♕f7+ ♔c8 32 ♕a7 ♖e8 33 ♖c1+ ♔d8 34 ♕b7 resigns**

Confusing right? Without explanations of the moves, this game remains a mysterious, fascinating mess. This is where good annotations reward the student.

Topalov – Gulko
Dos Hermanas 1994

White to play

We'll start here. Black has just retreated his well-placed bishop from a4 to b5. Why?

Once again it's a matter of targets. He doesn't want his kingside to come under fire from White's queen and bishops – as it would after 16 ... 0-0 17 ♘b3 ♖fc8 18 ♕g4.

Instead, he prefered **16 ... ♗b5** and the middlegame of 17 ♗xb5 axb5. Then he can target c2 with ... 0-0 and ... ♖fc8.

White considered a sacrifice, 17 a4 and then 17 ... ♗xa4 18 ♗a3, to discourage Black from castling. He didn't mind 17 ... ♗xd3 18 cxd3 because his c2 target disappears. But he rejected the sacrifice because 17 ... ♗xa4 18 ♗a3 ♕c3! threatens both 19 ... ♕xa3 and the queen-trading 19 ... ♕xd3!.

However, those variations didn't discourage White from sacrificing. White appreciated that his light-squared bishop has a lot more to do than his QR. That explains **17 ♖xb5!** and **17 ... axb5 18 ♕e2**.

Black to play

How risky is this? When you look at the coming ♗xb5, the answer is not much. If White gets to capture on b5 he will nearly have material equality.

In addition, he has good squares for his pieces after, say, 18 ... 0-0 19 ♗xb5 ♕c7 20 ♘b3 followed by 21 a4 and 22 ♗a3. Black's rooks wouldn't have an open file ('The rooks can't behave like rooks').

This helps explain why Black replied **18 ... ♖a4!**. It's an ideal counter-sacrifice. The material equality of 19 ♗xb5 ♕xc2 20 ♗xa4 ♕xa4 is fine for him.

And when White refused to accept the counter-sack, with **19 ♘b3!**, Black insisted with **19 ... ♖c4!**. It's easy to see how well Black stands after 20 ♗xc4? bxc4.

But White wasn't done. He ignored the rook once more and played **20 ♗d2**.

Black to play

His idea is to continue 21 ♗b4 and 22 c3. Then his least useful piece will be his knight and he can get rid of it profitably with ♘d2 and ♘xc4 For example, 20 ... 0-0? 21 ♗b4 ♖e8 22 c3 and 23 ♘d2. Black can't counter-sacrifice with 22 ... ♖xc3 because of 23 ♗xb5!.

From the diagram, play continued **20 ... ♘f5! 21 ♗b4!** (and not 21 c3? 0-0 when Black's king is safe and he would stand well). The position was clarified by **21 ... ♘xd4 22 ♘xd4 ♖xd4 23 ♗xb5 ♕c8**.

White's bishops are impressive but his chances seem doubtful in view of 24 ♗d6 ♖e4 followed by 25 ♕d2 ♖xe1+ and ... ♕xc2. Then Black can begin to squeeze out of the pressure with ... ♔d8 or ... ♕e4.

White to play

But **24 ♖d1!** made White's compensation clearer. After 24 ... ♖xd1+ 25 ♕xd1 and 26 c4 his attack would become overwhelming.

Instead, Black made one more Exchange sacrifice, **24 ... ♖xb4 25 axb4 ♕c3** to stop c2-c4. But there was another target, at g7.

After **26 ♕g4!** and then **26 ... ♕xe5 27 c4!** Black's position was too loose, e.g. 27 ... ♔e7 28 cxd5 ♘f6 29 ♕xg7 ♖g8 30 d6+!.

He lost after **27 ... f5 28 ♕g6+ ♔e7 29 cxd5 exd5 30 ♗xd7 ♔xd7 31 ♕f7+ ♔c8 32 ♕a7 and 33 ♖c1+**.

Quiz

42

Estrin – Spassky
Riga 1951

Black to play

Should Black play 1 ... ♕h4 and 2 g3 ♗xg3 ?

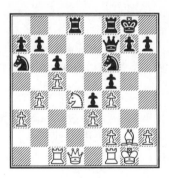

43
Ignatiev – Bronstein
Kislovodsk 1968

White to play

What do you think of 1 ♕e2?. It prevents ... ♕h5/ ... ♘g4/ ... ♖h6 and prepares for b4-b5.

44
Vaganian – Spassky
Moscow 1975

Black to play

Is a sacrifice on d4 sound?

45
Glek – Mikhalchishin
Zurich 2001

White to play

Evaluate and compare 1 ♗b4 and 1 ♖e4. Which is better?

46
Alekhine – Euwe
Match, Amsterdam 1926

White to play

What happens if White plays 1 ♗h4 ? Who is better if both sides find the best moves?

47
Zaharevic – Guliev
St. Petersburg 1997

White to play

Does Black have compensation for his pawn? And what should White do about it?

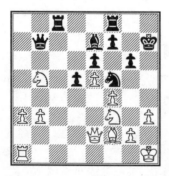

48
Ciolac – Gheorghiu
Rumanian Championship
1982

Black to play

White has given up the Exchange for two pawns. Does he have other compensation – and what should Black do?

Chapter Nine:
Knowing

There is an information gap that separates masters from the rest of players. But the information isn't arcane, technical material, like the best 17th move of a Najdorf Sicilian and how to draw ♖-vs.- ♖+♗.

The most valuable know-how that a master possesses and an amateur lacks concerns middlegame planning and pawn structures. A master knows what a good structure looks like, how to exploit it and when and how to change a structure that can be improved.

Smirin – D. Garcia
Las Palmas 1993

White to play

No threats and no easy targets. Not much seems to be happening, says the amateur.

The reality is quite different to a master. White can improve his position hugely with a few moves, starting with **1 ♘b5**.

This is another example of little tactics. White threatens ♘xd6 and perhaps also the a-pawn if he can drive Black's queen away.

Before playing 1 ♘b5 White had to make sure it wouldn't be refuted by 1 ... a6 2 ♘xd6 ♖fd8, pinning the knight. Once he saw that 3 ♘xb7 or 3 ♘xc8 ♖xd1 4 ♘xe7+ are good, he can be confident that 1 ♘b5 works tactically.

But this isn't about tactics. White didn't expect to win the d-pawn. He assumed Black would defend it, which he did, with **1 ... ♖fd8**. White's reasoning became clearer after the game continued **2 ♗d2 ♕a6**.

White to play

Most amateurs – and masters as well – would be looking at the discovered attacks on the queen, such as 3 ♘c7 or 3 ♘d4.

But it turns out that there's no way to win material, and 3 ♘c7 ♛c6 4 ♘xe6 fxe6 5 ♗d3 ♘bd7, for example, isn't a clear edge for White.

When White decided on 1 ♘b5! he also had a positional goal: He wanted to push his c-pawn to the fourth rank. That would create a very favorable pawn structure, a very good version of the Maroczy Bind. It is called a bind because it virtually rules out Black's main sources of counterplay, the advances ... b5 and ... d5.

Black couldn't stop this plan, so the game continued **3 b3! ♘bd7 4 c4!**.

Black to play

No Black counterplay means no White urgency, as we saw in Chapter Five. White has time to favorably reorganize his pieces. For example, he might continue ♗c1 and ♘d2, so that the a-pawn and e-pawn are protected. Then he can expand with b3-b4 and ♘c3-d5!.

In the game, Black tried to thwart that with **4 ... ♘c5**, threatening the e-pawn. But after White replied **5 ♘c3**, Black saw that 5 ... ♛xa3 would lose to 6 b4, e.g. 6 ... ♘cd7 7 ♖a1 ♛xb4 8 ♘d5.

To avoid a positional rout, he tried **5 ... b5**. But this made matters worse and he was lost soon after **6 b4! ♘cd7 7 cxb5 ♛xa3 8 ♖e3!**. His queen is trapped and vulnerable to ♘d5 or ♘e1-c2.

Black lost after **8 ... ♗f8 9 ♘e1! ♘b6 10 ♘c2**. But the turning point occurred back at the first diagram when White realized he could achieve the Maroczy Bind structure and knew it would favor him greatly.

The first step towards obtaining a favorable pawn structure is simply knowing which structures are favorable. Here's another example.

Shirov – Hulak
Manila 1992

White to play

This structure is harder to evaluate. It doesn't fit into any of the familiar patterns. Black has more pawns in the center. But White's pawns do a better job of limiting enemy pieces.

This is a case where a pawn structure suggests a maneuver. White's dark-squared bishop can control the best diagonal on the board after ♗e3-f2-h4 or ♗d2-e1-h4. But there's a drawback to the bishop maneuver. On h4, the bishop no longer protects f4. The f-pawn would become Black's best target, a source of counterplay.

So White looks for another plan. What do you do when you can't exploit the pawn structure? Change it to a better one. White played **1 c4!**.

His advantage would be evident after 1 ... dxc4 2 ♕xc4. A target at e6 is exposed and vulnerable to ♖d6 and ♘g5. Black can't maintain a pawn on d5 because 1 ... ♕f7? allows 2 ♘g5!.

That leaves 1 ... d4, which White realized was a distinctly favorable structure. True, Black will have a protected passed d-pawn. But once again this is a case of what matters most. White can exploit the hole at d6 with ♘g5-e4-d6. Or, after ♘g5, he can attack the kingside with ♖a3-h3 and ♕e4.

So play went **1 ... d4 2 ♘g5! ♘b8 3 ♖a3! ♘c6 4 ♖h3 h6 5 ♘e4**. White threatens to win with 6 ♕g4 and 7 ♕xg6, since 6 ... ♕f7 walks into 7 ♘d6!.

Black prepared to sacrifice a rook for the knight with 6 ... ♖ad8. White added more firepower with **7 ♖dd3**.

Black to play

Thanks to his highly favorable structure, White has a choice of winning methods. He can double rooks on g-file. Or he can grab material with ♘d6. He opted for the latter and **Black resigned** soon after **7 ... ♕f7 8 ♗d2 b6 9 axb6 axb6 10 ♘d6 ♖xd6 11 exd6**.

Good and Bad

Students don't pay much attention to pawn structures when they are starting out. They don't have to. They usually play standard openings, such as the Ruy Lopez, Queen's Gambit Declined, Giuoco Piano, and the Sicilian, Nimzo-Indian, King's Indian and Queen's Indian Defenses, and so on.

Each of these leaves you off, after 10 or so moves, with a more or less familiar pawn structure that is also more or less even. But when the middlegame begins, the structure begins to matter because either side can change it. A master not only knows what a good one looks like, but what to do about a bad one.

Topalov – Bareev
Dortmund 2002

White to play

This structure is typical, at least in terms of the center pawns, of a Caro-Kann Defense and of some queenside openings. White enjoys more space but both his d-pawn and h-pawn can become targets. This explains **1 ♕e5**.

White sees that 1 ... ♕xe5 2 dxe5 would transform the position into quite a nice structure for him. In fact, 2 ... ♖xd1+? 3 ♖xd1 and 4 ♖d7 would be close to losing for Black.

Black understood this and answered 1 ♕e5 with **1 ... ♕d8!**. He prepares, among other things, the pawn-killing plan of 2 ... ♕d7 followed by 3 ... ♖fd8 and 4 ... ♖xd4.

There is no way for White to change the structure in his favor after 1 ... ♕d8! because 2 d5? would just drop a pawn. So White provided support for his d-pawn with **2 ♖d3**.

Black to play

Now he can defend his d-pawn as many times as Black can attack it (2 ... ♛d7 3 ♖hd1). That's important: If there are no changes in the center, time begins to favor White. He would be free to turn his attention to the kingside where f3-f4 and g2-g4-g5! would give him a big edge.

But Black's last move prepared another plan. He assured himself of a superior pawn structure with **2 ... b5!**.

The tactical point is that 3 cxb5 allows 3 ... ♖d5! and 4 ... cxb5. Then Black has secured the pivotal d5 square, and the d4-pawn will remain a target for the foreseeable future (4 ♛f4 cxb5 5 g4? e5). No better is 3 c5 ♖d5.

White appreciated that keeping pawn control of d5 mattered more than loosening his king position. That led to **3 b3 bxc4 4 bxc4 ♛e7 5 ♔c2 ♖fd8**.

It's isn't easy to exploit White's king. But as we saw in Chapter Seven, in positions like this, it should be much easier to play Black's position than White's. Black eventually won after **6 ♛c5 ♖8d7 7 ♖hd1 ♛h4 8 g4 f6 9 ♛b4 f5!**.

Note how often the structure provides a hint about priorities, about what matters most. A favorable structure can serve as a virtual roadmap in the middlegame. Here's a memorable example.

Larsen – Tal
Leningrad 1973

Black to play

Black knew he enjoyed the superior pawn structure, particularly in view of the weakening h2-h4. This told him that White's threat – ♛xa7 – may not be worth preventing. The a-pawn shouldn't be as significant as one of White's kingside pawns, should it?

It shouldn't. Black considered **1 ... ♖fe8! 2 ♕xa7 ♖d6** and liked what he saw. The rook on d6 defends the b6-pawn and will go to f6 for an attack on f2.

In addition, he threatens 3 ... ♖xe2. White can't defend that pawn without major concessions (3 e4? fxe3 or 3 ♔f1 ♖f6 and 4 ... ♕f5).

Instead, he tried to open lines for his rooks with **3 b4**. But Black ignored that, too, with **3 ... ♖f6!**.

There followed **4 bxc5? ♕f5 5 f3** (or 5 ♖f1? ♖xe2 and 6 ... ♖xf2) **♕h3 6 ♕c7 ♖ff5!**.

White to play

Black wants to plant a rook on e5. That would block the c7-g3 diagonal and threaten a winning ... ♕xg3+. White's king has no escape because 7 ♔f2 will allow ... ♕h2+.

The finish was instructive. After **7 cxb6 ♖fe5 8 e4** Black coordinated his heavy pieces, **8 ... ♕xg3+ 9 ♔h1 ♕xh4+ 10 ♔g2 ♖g5+**. **White resigned** after **11 ♔f1 ♕h3+ 12 ♔e2 ♖g2+ 13 ♔d1 ♕xf3+ 14 ♔c1 ♕f2**.

It was very neatly done by Black and, since this occurred in an Interzonal tournament, the game played a role in chess history. It doomed one of Bent Larsen's last chances to become world champion.

The outcome was influenced by what happened several moves before the previous diagram. That is, before the pawn structure turned sharply in Black's favor. Here's what it looked like then.

Black to play

The first thing you'll notice is that there were two knights on the board. That seems to benefit White, even though both are pinned.

One reason they help White is that he has an additional piece to defend his kingside. In addition, he can trade knights on d4 under much better circumstances than what happened in the game.

For example, if Black plays the hasty 1 ... e5 White can reply 2 e4!, forcing the queen back before ♘xd4. For example, 2 ... ♕d6 3 ♘xd4! exd4 isn't nearly as good for Black as it was when the White pawn was on e2. Black would have no target on the e-file and White can defend f2 more easily.

This explains why Black played **1 ... ♖ad8!**. Now if 2 e4 and a queen retreat, Black can recapture on d4 with pieces and leave White to defend a backward pawn at d3 forever. For example, 2 ... ♕c6 3 ♘xd4 ♖xd4 and ... ♖fd8 is a clear edge for Black, thanks to the pawn structure.

Instead of 2 e4?, White played **2 ♔g1**. This unpins the knight so he can play 3 ♘xd4, not fearing 3 ... cxd4 4 ♕c4 or 4 ♕a3, or 3 ... ♕xd4 4 ♕xd4. Black would have only a minimal edge, if any.

Black also unpinned, with **2 ... e5** and threatened 3 ... ♘xf3+. White didn't like retreating his knight because his kingside has no defender, e.g. 3 ♘d2 g5! and 4 hxg5 hxg5 and ... ♖h8.

So there followed **3 ♘xd4 exd4! 4 ♕c4 ♕h5**.

White to play

We are nearly back to where we were in the first diagram we examined. But White still had a chance to make a fight of it through astute use of the pawn structure. Instead of 5 ♕a4?, which he played, he should liquidate one of his weaknesses with 5 e4!.

True, after 5 ... dxe3 6 ♖xe3 he still has to worry about the pawn at d3. But his rooks will become active, unlike in the game, and he has plenty of operating space. That matters more.

After he played **5 ♕a4?** and Black found **5 ... ♖d6!**, the game was largely decided.

175

Structured Study

How do you master pawn structures? The simplest way is to go over annotated games with different structures and figure out which structures are good, which are bad and which fall in between.

It's important to work with annotated games because good notes – that is, notes with words, not just moves – reveal a lot of subtleties you might otherwise miss.

**Vachier-Lagrave –
Nepomniachtchi**
Wijk aan Zee 2011

Black to play

You might be able to figure out on your own that White is slightly better and his advantage lies in the d5-pawn. It gives him more operating space than Black.

Black can try to change that evaluation with 1 ... ♘xb3 2 axb3 ♗xc3, threatening 3 ... ♕xd5. Or, he can tweak the move order with 1 ... ♗xc3 and then 2 bxc3 ♘xb3.

In the game, Black chose the latter. Without the benefit of notes you might not think it mattered.

It does. If Black had chosen **1 ... ♘xb3 2 axb3 ♗xc3** White would have been forced to save his d-pawn with **3 ♗xb6!** and then **3 ... ♕xb6 4 bxc3!**.

Black to play

If White is allowed to play 5 c4 he will have increased his edge appreciably because the structure is now plainly superior: He would have a target to pound at e7, the prospect of kingside attack with h2-h4-h5 and even the possibility of creating a passed queenside pawn.

Can Black change the structure? Yes, but he would be worse after 4 ... ♕xb3 5 ♖ab1 and ♖xb7. The same goes if Black tries to dissolve the d-pawn with 4 ... e6 5 dxe6 ♖xe6 6 ♖xe6 ♕xe6? 7 ♕xb7 or 6 ... fxe6 7 c4!.

But let's scroll back to the previous diagram. In the game Black actually played **1 ... ♗xc3!**. Then **2 bxc3 ♘xb3** forces **3 ♗xb6** once more.

Black to play

But in this version Black was able to insert the forcing **3 ... ♘d2!**. White wouldn't like to play 4 ♗xd8 ♘xf3+. So Black's trick allows him to equalize after 4 ♕d3 ♕xb6 5 ♕xd2 and now, for example, 5 ... ♖ad8 6 c4 e6!.

White, a good annotator, pointed all this out, as well as noting that he should have tweaked the move order as well – by meeting 1 ... ♗xc3! with 2 ♗xb6! and 2 ... ♕xb6 3 bxc3.

This makes sense because 3 ... ♘xb3 4 axb3 will have transposed into the favorable 1 ... ♘xb3 2 axb3 ♗xc3 line we mentioned above. (However, Black might have equalized anyway, by avoiding 3 ... ♘xb3? in favor of 3 ... ♕f6 or 3 ... ♕d6.)

Now if you had played the game score over without notes – and just saw 1 ... ♗xc3 2 bxc3 ♘xb3 3 ♗xb6 ♘d2 etc. – these subtleties would be lost and you would not be learning a valuable lesson about pawns.

Here's a more elaborate example. The two players take turns trying to get a structure they want to play. Without good notes the would-be master could get quite confused. He would realize how often the structure changes but not why.

Razuvaev – Sveshnikov, Moscow 1995: **1 d4 d5 2 c4 e6 3 ♘f3 c6 4 ♘bd2 ♘f6 5 g3 ♘bd7 6 ♕c2 b5**

Razuvaev – Sveshnikov
Moscow 1995

White to play

Black's last move tries to force a favorable trade, 7 cxb5 cxb5. That would likely allow him to seize the open file with ... ♖c8. Also ... ♗b7 after the pawn trade would make it hard for White to carry out his best bet (e2-e4) for opening the position in his favor.

White appreciated all this and played **7 c5!**. The new structure favors him. Why? Because he has more space and can open lines favorably for his pieces with either e2-e4 or a2-a4, or both.

Black saw this much too. He replied **7 ... e5** ("Otherwise I'm just positionally bad," he said afterwards).

The little tactic that makes 7 ... e5 possible is 8 dxe5 ♘g4, after which he must regain either the pawn at e5 or the one at c5.

So far, we've seen three tries at obtaining a better structure, 6 ... b5, 7 c5 and 7 ... e5. After **8 dxe5 ♘g4** White considered one more change, 9 e6 and 9 ... fxe6.

Black's position would be loosened and there would be potential targets at e6 and h7. But White couldn't see a way to exploit them in the near future.

Instead, he solidified his superior queenside with **9 b4!**.

Black to play

Left unchallenged, this move would allow White to create a bind with 10 ♗b2 and ♘b3-a5.

Black's pieces would be in such a mess that he might try to break out with 9 ... a5 before White has time for ♘b3.

But White could then sacrifice a pawn favorably, 10 ♗b2! axb4, in order to play 11 h3. After 11 ... ♘h6 his compensation lies in the positional pull of 12 ♘b3 and a later e2-e4. Or, after 12 ... ♗e7, in the tactics of 13 e6! ♘f6 14 g4.

Black appreciated as well as White did that the e5-pawn is the most important feature of these lines. He hurried to get it off the board with **9 ... ♘dxe5**, rather than 9 ... a5.

But, strangely enough, this was a mistake. (Correct was with 9 ... ♘gxe5!.)

The difference between the two captures was shown by **10 ♗b2 ♘xf3+ 11 exf3!**.

Black to play

Black had counted on 11 ♘xf3 so that he could anticipate 12 a4 with 11 ... a5!. Then his queenside inferiority is reduced.

But after 11 exf3! his knight is under attack and White has time to deter ... a5. Play went **11 ... ♘f6 12 ♘b3!**.

The doubling of White's pawns isn't nearly as important as his ability to solidify on the queenside. He can complete his development and then make inroads with a2-a4 and/or ♘a5. Or he can try to attack on the kingside with ♗d3.

Black knew from his own experience how bad positions like 12 ... ♗e7 13 a4 bxa4 14 ♖xa4 are. He became desperate and tried **12 ... a5**.

He planned to sacrifice with 13 ♘xa5 ♖xa5 14 bxa5 ♕xa5+ 15 ♕d2 ♕xd2+ 16 ♔xd2 ♗xc5 or 15 ♗c3 ♕a3.

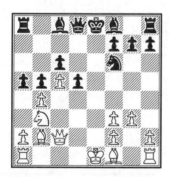

White to play

But White has one more favorable way to alter the pawns, **13 a4!**, rather than 13 ♘xa5. Then 13 ... bxa4 14 ♖xa4 would doom the a5-pawn without any compensation. Instead, Black chose **13 ... axb4 14 axb5 ♖xa1+ 15 ♗xa1**.

If Black allows 16 b6, the protected passed pawn leaves him positionally lost. But Black would lose even faster after 15 ... cxb5 16 ♗xb5+ ♗d7 17 c6.

The game drew to a finish after **15 ... ♗e7 16 b6! 0-0 17 h4**. White is taking minor precautions, to avoid complications such as 17 ♗d3 ♗h3 or 17 ♗g2 ♗a6.

After Black tried **17 ... d4 18 ♗c4 ♘d5 19 ♗xd4 ♖e8**, White took another safety step, **20 ♔f1!**, to avoid the complications of 20 0-0 ♗xh4!?.

179

But the game had been decided earlier by clever pawn play. The bankruptcy of Black's position was clear after **20 ... ♗f6 21 ♗xf6 ♛xf6 22 ♗xd5 cxd5 23 ♔g2** and the queenside pawns must win.

Pawns and Priyomes

Obtaining the pawn structure you want to play is typically the first step of a two-step process. The equally important second step is knowing how to exploit it. The Russians gave us a word – *priyome* – to describe the technique that is appropriate for a particular pawn structure.

You already know some of these even if you've never heard of the word priyome. Suppose you're playing a rook endgame with seven pawns apiece. There is one open file. The priyome is simply to seize control of the file with your rook. It's virtually an automatic, no-think move for most players and it typically obtains an advantage.

Most priyomes are much more sophisticated than that. They are both tactical and strategic. They can provide you with just a hint of what the next move should be. Or they can hand you a full-blown middlegame script, leading almost to mate. Here's an elaborate priyome that became familiar in the last 20 years and defeated some of the strongest players.

Kasparov – Anand
Linares 1994

White to play

Knowing the priyome allows White to play his next half dozen moves with confidence. He begins with **1 g4!**.

If allowed, he will continue 2 g5 followed by 3 ♗g2, to free the rook at f1. Then comes 4 ♖f3 and 5 ♖h3, targeting h7. He follows up by getting his queen to the h-file and threatening ♛xh7 mate.

This plan is so strong that if Black doesn't take emergency action – say with 1 ... d5!? 2 exd5 ♖d8 – he can be overrun. In fact, the priyome begun by 1 g4 has won hundreds of games, in similar positions. Often Black has to do all the hard thinking – because White is being guided by the priyome.

This game illustrated this when it continued **1 ... ♖b8? 2 g5 ♞d7 3 ♗g2! ♖e8 4 ♖f3 ♞c5? 5 ♖h3**. To stop 6 ♛h5, Black played **5 ... g6**. White replied **6 ♛g4**.

Black to play

The script goes much further: Black cannot stop ♕h4. But he has a trick defense to it in ... h5, since gxh6 would lose the queen to ... ♗xh4.

Nevertheless White will win if he is allowed to play ♗f3xh5!. That's what happened here: **6 ... ♘b4? 7 ♕h4 h5 8 ♗f3! ♗f8 9 ♗xh5 gxh5 10 ♕xh5 ♗g7** and now **11 ♗d4! e5 12 f5!** (12 ... exd4 13 ♕h7+ ♔f8 14 f6).

There have been dozens of master games that began with g2-g4 and ended with Black resigning soon after ♗xh5!. One of them is the following, which arose from quite a different opening variation.

Fedorov – Khurtsidze, Krasnodar 1998: **1 e4 c5 2 ♘f3 e6 3 d4 cxd4 4 ♘xd4 a6 5 ♘c3 ♕c7 6 g3 ♗b4 7 ♗d2 ♘f6 8 ♗g2 ♘c6 9 ♘b3 ♗e7 10 f4 d6 11 0-0 0-0 12 g4! b5 13 g5 ♘d7 14 a3 ♗b7 15 ♖f3 ♖fe8 16 ♖h3 g6 17 ♕e1 b4 18 ♕h4 h5**

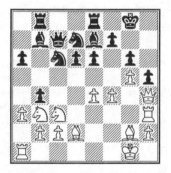

Fedorov – Khurtsidze
Krasnodar 1998

White to play

The first move to occur to Sicilian-beating masters is obvious, **19 ♗f3!**. The game was decided by **19 ... bxc3 20 ♗xh5!** since 20 ... gxh5 21 ♕xh5 leads to immediate mate.

Black kept the game going with **20 ... ♗xg5 21 ♕xg5 ♕d8** but resigned soon after **22 ♕h6! cxb2 23 ♖f1 ♕f6 24 ♗c3**.

Priyomes and pawn structures are intimately related. Changing the pawn structure, as White did with g2-g4-g5, will make little sense unless you know the priyome that is appropriate. A change in structure also lacks point if you don't have the pieces to make the priyome work. Sometimes a pawn advance or capture can be a brilliant move or a positional blunder depending on whether you can carry out the priyome.

P. Nikolic – Kramnik
Monte Carlo 1998

Black to play

White is preparing the familiar minority attack, with b4-b5 followed by bxc6 to weaken Black's pawns.

Black stopped that plan in the most direct way, with 1 ... b5. He explained this is a "very typical move" in this kind of position.

But he added that it's *only* good if Black can maneuver a knight to c4. That's the priyome. In this case it's a very short range plan that lasts only until Black plays ... ♘c4.

If he can't plug the c-file that way, Black will be clearly worse. He will find the backward c6-pawn coming under heavy fire from rooks on the c-file, and the conclusion to draw is that 1 ... b5? was a positional blunder.

But in this case, Black can get his knight to c4 and **1 ... b5!** was the most important move in the game. Play went **2 ♕c2 axb4 3 axb4 ♘d6! 4 ♖b3 ♘b6 5 ♘e5 ♖fc8 6 ♘d3 ♘bc4** and he was better. He went on to win a fine game.

Counter-Priyome

Some priyomes are so sophisticated that they have inspired specific antidotes – a kind of counter-priyome. Here's a pair of illustrations. In the first case the priyome succeeds perfectly. In the second it is foiled by a counter-priyome.

Spassky – Zuk
Vancouver 1971

White to play

We see a typical King's Indian/Benoni pawn structure. There are no obvious targets for either player. But White detected a slight Black weakness on the kingside in the vicinity of g6 and f6. That was enough to start calculating variations.

First, he could see that he lacks the firepower to make 1 e5 dxe5 2 fxe5 ♕xe5 work. Even if prepared with 1 ♖de1, the e4-e5 break is going to cost a pawn, with little to show for it.

White also looked at 1 f5. That threatens to target g6 and create a hole at e6 with 2 fxg6 fxg6.

But 1 f5 is also a major concession, granting Black a wonderful outpost at e5. For example, 1 ... g5 2 ♗g3 ♘d7! and ... ♘e5.

Nevertheless White knew there should be something to do here because he knew his priyomes: He needs to clear e4 for his knights. After some calculation he found that the proper way to do that is **1 ♗xf6! ♗xf6 2 e5!** and then **2 ... dxe5 3 ♘e4 ♗g7**.

White to play

But the priyome goes beyond what's happened so far. After an exchange of White's f-pawn or Black's e-pawn, Black will have lots of piece activity, e.g. 5 fxe5? ♕xe5 6 ♘2c3 ♕d4+ favors Black.

The key move is **5 f5!**, which guarantees White an advantage. By stopping ... f5 he secured e4 for his knight. White also prepares to probe the kingside with ♘2c3 followed by ♕g3/f5-f6. Or, after 5 ... g5, with 6 f6 and ♘2g3-f5.

Play went **5 ... ♖d8 6 ♘2c3 gxf5 7 ♖xf5**. White is preparing ♘f6+, with or without a rook lift, ♖df1-f3-g3 or -h3. **7...f6**

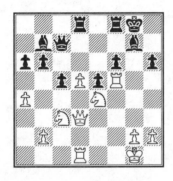

White to play

Black felt he had to play 7 ... f6. This makes it hard for either player to change the structure further. But it's a very favorable structure for White – and time is on his side because Black has little counterplay.

The way White finished off was instructive: **8 ⬜df1 ♛e7 9 ♛g3 ♚h8 10 ♛h4 ♝xd5 11 ♘xf6 ♝b7 12 ⬜h5! ⬜xf6 13 ⬜xh6+! ♚g8** (13 ... ♝xh6 14 ⬜xf6 wins) **14 ⬜fxf6! ♝xf6** (or 14 ... ♝xh6 15 ♛xh6 and ⬜g6+ wins) **15 ⬜xf6** and so on.

The priyome here consists mainly of 2 e5!, 3 ♘e4 and 5 f5!. It became famous when a world champion was wiped out in the game Penrose – Tal, Leipzig 1960. That game and the one above have little in common except for a few pawns in the center and the priyome.

The would-be master will want to master this priyome because it arises so often. He can find dozens of games in Benoni and King's Indian Defense databases. What he wants to learn is: When does the e4-e5 followed by f4-f5 succeed and how can it fail? He also wants to see if there are any good defenses to it.

In fact, there is a counter-priyome, and it was illustrated by another Spassky game, played about the same time as the one above.

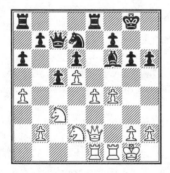

Spassky – Balashov
Moscow 1971

White to play

White has just exchanged a bishop for a knight on f6, as he did in the previous example. Yes, there are differences between the two games. But the similarities are more important. They included White's ability to control e4 with his knights, Black's weakness at g6 and the potential outpost at f5.

That explains **1 e5! dxe5 2 f5**. White is ready to carry out the same pressure plan as before, by means of ♘de4 with its a threat of fxg6/ ♘xf6+.

As in the previous example, he is trying to force Black to trade pawns on f5 so that he can retake ⬜xf5 and dominate the f-file.

Once again, 2 ... g5, invites ♘de4, this time with d5-d6 and ♘d5 to come, an idea that was possible but impractical in the previous example.

Black to play

The strength of the priyome is illustrated by a sample variation that begins 2 ... ♗g7 3 ♘de4 ♔h7 (not 3 ... ♘f6 4 ♘xf6+ ♗xf6 5 fxg6, threatening ♖xf6).

White would be getting close to a win after 4 ♕g4 in view of 4 ... ♖f8 5 f6 ♗h8 6 ♕h4 and ♘g5+. Or 4 ... ♕d8 5 fxg6+ fxg6 6 ♖f7.

But there was a counter-priyome that Black knew about and he replied **2 ... e4!**. This enabled him to occupy e5, which Black never managed to do in the previous example. Once again it's a case of what matters most. Black appreciates that the loss of his extra pawn doesn't mean as much as having room for his pieces to work.

There followed **3 fxg6 fxg6 4 ♘dxe4 ♔g7!** and Black has protected key squares at g6 and f6.

White to play

White still has good play but Black had plenty of resources when the game continued **5 ♔h1** and **5 ... ♖e5! 6 ♕d2 ♖ae8**. A draw was the fair result following **7 g3 ♖f5 8 ♖xf5 gxf5 9 ♘xf6 ♖xe1+ 10 ♕xe1 ♘xf6**.

Mastering Priyomes

It's harder to acquire a good appreciation of priyomes than it is to master pawn structures. For one thing, there are many more priyomes than structures. Often a single structure can have two or three priyomes, as in the last example. This applies to attack as much as it does to positional play.

185

Rublevsky – Goloshchapov
Silviri 2003

White to play

The hanging c- and d-pawns and the related d4-isolani are two of the most common pawn structures. Both offer White reason to be aggressive.

One of his priyomes is the explosive d4-d5. When White is better developed, this can give him a quick advantage. But here the tactics don't justify 1 d5? exd5 2 ♗xd5 ♗b7. Black is at least equal.

Another priyome is the unlikely **1 h4!**. White's idea is to support ♘g5, which will be followed by ♕h5, to threat mate on h7. As strange as it may seem, it is quite common in positions with the same or similar pawn structures.

To play 1 h4 White has to realize it is a gambit, 1 ... ♗xh4 2 ♘xh4 ♕xh4 – and that it's a promising gambit after 3 ♖e3, with the idea of ♖h3/♗c2 or ♖g3/♗g5.

Should Black accept the pawn? That depends on his alternatives. If he stops 2 ♘g5 with 1 ... h6, White will play 2 ♕d3 and 3 ♗c2, forcing another weakening to avert mate on h7.

In the game Black chose **1 ... ♗b7 2 ♘g5** and saw that 2 ... h6 allows a strong 3 ♘xe6! fxe6 4 ♖xe6. So he played **2 ... ♘a5** instead and then came **3 ♗c2**.

Black to play

The power of 1 h4! is now evident. If Black meets the ♗xh7+ threat with 3 ... g6, White can prepare h4-h5xh6 or go straight into a standard sacrifice – another priyome – 4 ♘xh7 ♔xh7 5 ♕h5+ ♔g8 6 ♗xg6.

Black chose **3 ... ♗xg5** instead. But his kingside dark squares were a chronic weakness after **4 hxg5** and then **4 ... ♗d5 5 ♕d3! g6 6 ♕g3**, followed by ♗f4, ♖ad1-d3 and ♕h4.

Amateurs can play some positions well because they learned, often unconsciously, the appropriate priyomes. Masters can play many positions well because they know more of them.

"I think my advantage as a practical player," said Hikaru Nakamura in a 2011 interview, lies in that "I play a great many positions. Even the best (opening) preparation at some moment comes to an end and then you need to fight."

Here's how to look at a game and add to your knowledge of structures and priyomes:

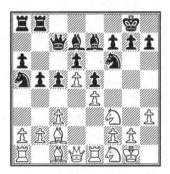

Livshin – Geller
Kiev 1954

White to play

This is a standard Ruy Lopez middlegame structure. You can find thousands of games with these pawns on these squares, although the pieces may be placed differently.

If you search for similar games in databases, you'll appreciate the basic themes. Black is trying to open up the queenside, where he has more space. Often he tries ... c4, ... a5 and then ... b4xc3.

Meanwhile, White eyes the kingside. One priyome that you'll find is to play a White knight to e3, his king to h2, his rook to g1 and then advance the g-pawn two squares. The priyome is completed when White gets his knight to f5. That's a powerful attacking setup and has been examined in, for example, *Pawn Power in Chess* by Hans Kmoch.

But there's also a matter of move order. White can start with ♔h2 and ♘e3, followed by ♖g1/g2-g4 or g2-g4/♖g1. However, he chose the sloppy **1 g4?**.

That gave Black an opportunity to carry out his own priyome with **1 ... h5** – even though he seems to be attacking on the wing in which he is weaker. If you examine databases you'll find similar examples that lead to double-edged play. In some rare cases White stands better after gxh5 and ... ♗xh3. Knowing the priyome only gives you a likely candidate. It doesn't guarantee you the best move.

This time **1 ... h5!** is good. Black would stand well after 2 g5 ♘h7! 3 ♔h2 ♕d8 because the g-pawn is overextended. White preferred **2 ♘3h2** and Black traded pawns, **2 ... hxg4 3 hxg4**.

Black to play

The kingside pawn structure is somewhat rare but once again there's a priyome, **3 ... ♘h7!** and ... ♘g5 or ... ♗g5. It puts Black in excellent shape to exploit the dark-square holes on the kingside. Play continued **4 ♘e3 g6!**.

If you're not familiar with this kind of position, you might think it is fairly equal. It isn't. And because White didn't appreciate that, he didn't feel he needed to defend.

There is a good defensive try and it can be considered – guess what? – another priyome. White should fortify his kingside with 5 f3! followed by ♔g2 and ♖h1.

Instead he felt he could still attack if he got f2-f4 in. The game continued **5 ♘g2? ♘g5 6 b3 ♔g7! 7 f4 exf4 8 ♘xf4 ♖h8 9 ♗d3 ♖h4 10 ♘g2 ♖h7**.

White to play

Black has the better pieces and the only targets to aim at. White tried to stem the tide with **11 ♗xg5 ♗xg5 12 ♗e2 ♗f6 13 ♖c1**. But it was too late and **13 ... c4!** opened up the diagonal leading to his king. There followed **14 ♘e3 cxb3 15 axb3 ♖ah8**.

A pretty finish would have been 16 ♘ef1 ♕c5+ 17 ♔g2 and now 17 ... ♖xh2+! 18 ♘xh2 ♖xh2+! 19 ♔xh2 ♕f2+ and ... ♗e5 with a mate.

Instead, White played **16 ♘f3 ♕b6 17 ♘d4** and could have resigned after either 17 ... ♖h1+ 18 ♔g2 ♖8h2+ 19 ♔f3 ♗h4 or 19 ... ♖h3+ 20 ♔g2 ♖xe1 and ... ♖xe3.

And now for our final set of quiz positions.

Quiz

49
Bu Xiangzhi – Acs
Peristeri 2001

Black to play

Where does Black's counterplay lie and how should he get it moving?

50
Timman – Berg
Malmo 2001

White to play

Is the pawn structure good for White and what should he do about it?

51
Yates – Capablanca
Moscow 1925

Black to play

Who wants to change the pawn structure? What should Black do?

52
Tseitlin – Avrukh
Beershiva 1999

White to play

Black has allowed a tactical priyome. Which one?

Quiz Answers

1. The most important feature is the superiority of White's minor pieces over Black's. To maximize that edge White correctly traded rooks, **1 ♖xe8+! ♖xe8 2 ♖e1**.

If Black had continued 2 ... ♖xe1+ 3 ♗xe1 White would have continued ♗c3, ♔h2, ♗f3 and g3-g4 to drive the knights back. His edge in space would be nearly decisive.

Black foiled that plan by gaining an outpost at g3, with **2 ... h4**, and there followed **3 ♖xe8+ ♘xe8 4 g4 ♘g3 5 f5! ♘f6 6 ♗g5 ♕e8!**.

White to play

Black is offering a pawn in order to gain counterplay (7 ♗xh4 ♘e2+ and 8 ... ♘f4).

But White recognized that trading queens mattered more and played **7 ♕e3! ♕xe3+ 8 ♗xe3**. That left him with two bishops that have grown in power over the two knights because the heavy pieces are gone.

One of the reasons bishops are superior to knights is that they have an easier time forcing trades. White won by entering a pawn-ending, **8 ... a5 9 ♔f2 g5 10 ♔e1** (10 ♗xg5?? ♘fe4+) **10 ... ♘fe4 11 ♗xe4! ♘xe4 12 ♔e2 f6 13 ♔d3 ♘c5+** (13 ... ♘g3 14 ♗a7! and ♗b8) **14 ♗xc5! dxc5 15 ♔c3**.

2. As bad as Black's bishop is, it defends his weakest pawns, at f5, d5 and f7. After **1 ♘c7 ♖ag8 2 ♘xe6!** Black's position was riddled with permanent and vulnerable targets and he lost eventually following **2 ... ♔xe6** (3 ♖xg8 ♘xg8 4 ♔e2 ♘e7 5 ♔f3 and ♔f4).

3. White has attacking chances on the kingside but only if he keeps minor pieces, like his knight, on the board. Typical play is **1 ♘f3 ♘d5 2 0-0 ♗e7 3 ♘c3** and **4 ♖e1** with a slight edge for White.

191

On the other hand, 1 ♘xc6 weakens Black's pawns but the one at c6 is no weaker than the White one at d4.

4. Opening the a-file is Black's main source of counterplay. At the cost of a pawn, White kills it with **1 b5!**. Second in significance to closing the queenside is White's domination of the dark squares after 2 ♗a3!.

The game ended with **1 ... ♕xb5 2 ♗a3! b6 3 ♕h6 ♗b7** and now **4 ♖xg6+! hxg6 5 ♕xg6+ ♔h8 6 ♕xf7 ♖g8 7 ♗f8! resigns**, in view of 7 ... ♘xf8 8 ♘f6.

5. Yes, because **1 ... ♗xe5! 2 dxe5** allows him to obtain a superior pawn structure following **2 ... ♘ac5!**. A better pawn structure often matters much more than the fortunes of a single piece.

White's bishop on d3 is attacked and 3 ♗xe4 dxe4 would create a hole that Black can exploit with ... ♘d3. In addition, the e5-pawn may be lost.

White cannot defend the bishop with 3 ♕e2 because that allows 3 ... ♘xd2 4 ♕xd2 ♘b3. That leaves **3 ♗c2**, which Black met with **3 ... ♘xd2 4 ♕xd2 d4!**,

White to play

Black was obviously superior after **5 ♘a4 ♘b3! 6 ♗xb3 ♗xb3** and would have been winning after 5 ♘b5? d3! 6 ♗d1 ♘e4.

6. As Bobby Fischer put it, "to get squares you gotta give squares." Best is **1 c5!**, severely limiting Black's queen bishop and heavy pieces. Surrendering d5 is a lesser concern because it can be occupied by only one piece, and with no other counterplay (no ... c5!) White can expand on the queenside at will.

His method was instructive: **1 ... ♘d5 2 a3 a5 3 ♗f1 ♕c7 4 ♗d2 ♖fd8 5 b4 axb4 6 ♗xb4!**.

Now 6 ... ♘xb4?! gives up the best thing about Black's position. He preferred **6 ... ♖a8** but then came **7 cxb6 ♕xb6 8 ♗xe7 ♘xe7 9 ♘c5 ♗c8**.

There's a new priority in the position. What matters most is White's passed a-pawn. He won shortly after **10 a4! ♖a5 11 ♘b3 ♖ad5 12 a5 ♕a7 13 a6 ♗d7 14 ♗c4 ♖d6 15 ♘c5** followed by ♕b2 and ♖db1.

7. There are targets at f2 and a3. The first is more vulnerable and that means it takes precedence, **1 ... ♗b8!** and 2 ... ♗a7!.

Play went **2 ♖d2 ♗a7 3 ♖e1 ♖ac8** and the threat to exploit the second target with ... ♖c3 shortened matters.

After **4 ♘e3 ♘xe3 5 ♖d7+ ♖f7 6 ♖xf7+ ♔xf7 7 fxe3** Black can win a pawn with 7 ... ♖c3. But **7 ... ♖c1!** forces resignation in view of 8 ♖xc1 ♗xe3+. No better was 5 fxe3 ♗xe3+! 6 ♖xe3 ♖c1+ and mates.

8. Black's last move, ... ♗e6, left the b-pawn unprotected. White should attack it with **1 ♖a3!** and ♖b3.

Black would give his opponent control of good squares if he played 1 ... ♗xc4 2 ♕xc4 and create new targets if he played 1 ... ♕b4 2 ♗xe6 fxe6. Instead, he looked for kingside counterplay with **1 ... ♘h5** but after **2 ♗xe6 ♕xe6 3 ♖b3** White had carried out his plan effectively.

Black to play

Black must make concessions if he defends b7, e.g. as 3 ... ♕c6? 4 ♘d5!, which threatens 5 ♘e7+ as well as 5 ♖c3.

Black played the natural **3 ... ♖ab8** but **4 ♖d1!** created a new threat (5 ♖xd8+ ♖xd8 6 ♖xb7) and led to new concessions, **4 ... ♖xd1+ 5 ♕xd1 ♗f6 6 ♕d5!**.

Now 6 ... ♕xd5 7 ♘xd5 ♗d8 8 ♗a7 or, as the game went, **6 ... ♕c8 7 ♘a4!** and ♘c5 gives White a winning game.

9. There are four potential targets: h7, g7 and even b5 and c6.

The last two don't look remotely vulnerable. But after a3-a4 White can exploit the knight's presence on c4 by means of doubling rooks on the c-file followed by b2-b3.

But White should have something more convincing. The target at h7 is vulnerable to ♗b1 followed by either ♕c2 or ♕d3, with the threat of ♘f6+ and ♕h7 mate.

White chose to go after the fourth target, g7. He began with **1 h3! a4 2 ♘h2!**, intending ♘g4-f6+!. Black cannot capture on f6 without allowing White's queen to inflict fatal damage. Black avoided that with **2 ... f5** and then **3 exf6 ♗xf6 4 ♘xf6+ ♖xf6 5 ♖xf6 gxf6 6 ♘g4**.

Black to play

White either wins a pawn (6 ... ♕g7 7 ♕f3 followed by ♕xc6 or ♘xf6+) or gets a winning attack (6 ... ♔g7 7 ♘xf6! ♔xf6 8 ♖f1+ ♔e7 9 ♕h5).

10. White can't cash in his kingside pressure until he eliminates his targets (b2, c2) on the queenside. After 1 ♕xh7? he has to watch out for ... ♕c3.

With **1 c4!** and **1 ... bxc3 2 ♔c2!**, however, the targets are no longer a factor. White won after **2 ... ♔d8 3 ♕xh7 ♖f8 4 g5** followed by ♗g4 and h4-h5 etc.

11. His bishop looks good but needs to do more. The obvious target is e6. He played **1 ♗d3!** and headed it to g4.

Black has four pieces to defend the e-pawn, five if you include the king. But the defense is hard because of tactics (1 ... ♖e8? 2 ♗b5).

The game went **1 ... ♖c7 2 ♗e2 ♖c6 3 b4! ♕d8 4 b5 ♖d6?! 7 ♗g4 ♖f6** and White crashed through with **8 ♕a3!** (8 ... ♕c7 9 ♖c1 ♕-moves 10 ♖xc8!).

12. His knight isn't doing enough and blocks the rook. Instead of 1 ... ♕b2? 2 ♗xf5 ♕c3, which drew, Black should move the knight – to a3 or even d6 to clear c3 – **1 ... ♘d6!** threatens 2 ... ♖c3 as well as 2 ... ♘e4+, and **2 exd6 ♗xd6+ 3 ♔h4 ♕f2+ 4 ♔h5 ♖c3** would win.

13. White has a target at e5. Instead of calculating, he should visualize the best piece placement to attack the e-pawn. That indicates his queen on h2 and a shift of his knight to f3. The game went **1 ♗d3 a6 2 ♖dg1 ♕e7 3 ♕h2 ♗f6** and now **4 ♘b1! ♖g8 5 ♘d2 ♘f7**

White to play

Now is the time for White to calculate. He can't increase the pressure on e5 after 6 ♘f3. But he saw another idea, ♘f3-h4-g6+!.

That prompted him to work out a winning line, which began **6 ♘f3! e4 7 ♘h4 exd3 8 ♘g6+ hxg6 9 hxg6 + ♔g7 10 ♕h7+ ♔f8 11 gxf7**.

Black avoided that with **7 ... ♘h6** but eventually lost following **8 ♗e2 ♖g7 9 ♗d6**.

14. ♗d1 is a good idea but don't calculate it yet. White can visualize his way to an excellent game by getting a minor piece to the big hole at c6.

He can consider ♕b2 followed by ♘a2-b4-c6. But more promising is 1 ♗e2, which defends c4 and prepares 2 b4. Then, after the Black knight retreats, White has an impressive maneuver, ♗d1-a4-c6.

As the game went, **1 ♗e2! ♘d7 2 b4 ♘b7 3 ♗d1! f5 4 ♗a4 ♖f8 5 ♗c6 ♖b8**, White didn't have to calculate anything until he was ready to break through. He anticipated ... f4-f3 with 6 f3! and there followed **6 ... ♘f6 7 ♖fd1 ♘h5 8 ♕d2 ♖f7**.

White to play

Only now did White need to work out variations, and he won after **9 ♗xb7! ♖xb7 10 c5! bxc5 11 bxc5 dxc5** and then **11 d6 ♗f6 12 ♘a4 and ♘xc5**.

15. Both. The targets are at f7 and the hole at b6. Although his queen looks nice on c3 White will get much more out of it on f2, where it threatens ♗b6 and supports f4-f5.

After **1 ♕e1!** Black didn't like the looks of 1 ... ♖ac8 2 ♕f2 and 3 ♗b6.

He preferred **1 ... b6 2 ♕f2 ♖db8** but then came **3 f5!**, based on 3 ... exf5 4 ♗f4.

Black lost after **3 ... ♕c8 4 ♘d4 ♘xd4 5 ♗xd4 ♘c6** and now **6 fxe6! ♗xe6 7 ♗xe6 resigns**, in view of 7 ... ♕xe6 8 ♖xc6 ♕xc6 9 ♕xf7+ and mates.

16. White's biggest problem, surprisingly, is his knight on b5. It's "totally marooned," White said after the game. As long as it can't move, White's ability to open the file with bxc5 means little.

The solution is **1 ♘g5!**. White threatens 2 ♘xd4!, since after Black captures on d4 with a pawn, White plays 3 b5 followed by bxc6, exposing b6 as a target.

195

If Black avoids this with, say **1 ... h6**, he allows White's second idea, **2 ♘ge4** and **3 ♘ed6**, when the knights are doing something.

17. 1 ♗h3! secures an advantage positionally based on his control of light squares and **1 ... ♗xh3 2 ♕h5+ g6 3 ♕xh3**. (No better is **1 ... ♗f7 2 ♕g4!**).

There were more tactics after **3 ... ♘b6** and then **4 fxe5!**, so that 4 ... ♘xc4 5 exf6, with advantage. Worse for Black is 4 ... ♘xe5 5 ♘xe5 ♕xe5? 6 ♗f4 or 5 ... fxe5 6 ♕e6!.

Black had nothing better after 4 fxe5 than **4 ... fxe5** after which **5 ♕e6!** threatens ♕f7+ and led to **5 ... ♘xc4 6 ♕xc4 0-0-0**.

White to play

The way to exploit White's better pieces was **7 ♘f3!**, which threatens ♘g5-f7 and obtains a very favorable middlegame.

18. Did you forget the Grischuk – Giri position? The solution is **1 ♘e6!** because **1 ... fxe6 2 dxe6** regains material with its threat of 3 e7+.

But the main point is that White has gained positional plusses after **2 ... ♔h8 3 exd7 ♕xd7**. He has isolated Black's e-pawn, which restricts his only bishop. White built up his edge slowly (**4 0-0 ♕f5 5 ♘d5 ♘g8 6 ♕g4 ♕c7 7 ♕e2 ♕f5** and now 8 e4 and ♖ad1 put him clearly on top).

19. With the mate threat on h7, **1 ♘g5! ♗xg5 2 ♗xb7**.

After **2 ... ♖a7 3 ♗e4!** White has new threats, ♕xd6 and ♗xh7+. Black had to play **3 ... f5.**

But after **4 ♗g2 ♖d7 5 f4!** and 6 e4! White's edge had grown considerably, in view of Black's weaknesses on squares such as e6.

Black made it easy, **5 ... ♗f6 6 e4 ♗xc3 7 bxc3!? a5? 8 exf5 ♖xf5 9 ♗h3** and **Black resigned** in view of 9 ... ♖f6 10 ♗xe6+! ♖xe6 11 ♕d5 ♕f6 12 f5.

20. Yes, he deserves more in view of White's vulnerable king. It becomes much harder for White than for Black to find good moves after **1 ... ♕c8!**, with ideas such as ... ♕b7+, ... ♖d8 and later ... ♘e4.

Play went **2 ♕f2 ♕b7+** and White found **3 ♔g1!**, hoping for 3 ... ♕xb2 4 ♗e5! or 3 ... ♖d8 4 ♗g5!.

But it was relatively easy for Black to find strong replies such as ... ♘e4 and ... ♖e8-e6-g6, while White had to avoid tactical landmines.

The game went **3 ... ♘e4! 4 ♕d4 ♖e8** and turned in Black's favor after **5 ♖e2?! h6 6 h3 ♖e6! 7 ♔h2 f5 8 b4 ♔h7 9 ♖e3 ♖g6 10 ♖e2 ♕b5**.

He won an endgame after **11 ♖e1 ♖c6 12 ♖xe4 fxe4**.

21. You may have seen that 1 ♖xc8 and 2 ♗xe6+ wins a pawn. But you shouldn't have stopped there. The extra pawn doesn't make for an easy win in the rook ending.

Better is **1 ♖f1!** to maximize White's positional edge, as we'll discuss in Chapter Six. Since 1 ... ♖d8 or 1 ... ♖e8 allow 2 ♖ff7, Black had to trade his only active piece, **1 ... ♖xf1+**.

Then came **2 ♔xf1 ♔f8 3 ♔f2**.

Black to play

White threatens to keep marching his king, ♔e3-d4-c5. Black acknowledged the loss of a pawn – under much worse circumstances than 1 ♖xc8 – with **3 ... a5 4 ♖a7 ♖b6**. He would have lost quickly after 4 ... ♖b5 5 ♖a8 ♖c5 5 ♗xe6.

After 4 ... ♖b6 White again passed up the win of a pawn, 5 ♖a8 ♖c6 6 ♗xe6 ♖xe6 7 ♖xc8+. He prolonged the pressure with **5 ♗g2**, threatening 6 ♖a8.

Then came **5 ... ♗a6 6 b3** and Black had run out of useful moves. The game ended with **6 ... a4 7 bxa4 ♗c4 8 a5! ♖b5 9 ♖c7 ♗xa2 10 a6 ♖a5 11 a7**.

22. Don't give up on the idea. After **1 ... ♕xc3 2 ♗xd8** White's first rank is still vulnerable and if you look hard you might find **2 ... ♕f3!**, which wins (3 ♖xf3 ♖d1 mate or 3 ♖e1 ♖d1+).

White resigned after **3 ♗c7+ ♔xc7 4 ♕f7+ ♕xf7 5 ♖xf7+ ♖d7**, being a piece down.

23. Black doesn't have much after 1 ... ♗xd4 2 ♗xd4 ♕xd4 3 ♘ec2 ♕d3 4 ♕e7, intending ♕xe4.

Black shouldn't stop there. He should consider 1 ... ♘f5 because capturing on d4 with a knight is preferable. But 2 ♘ec2 ♘xd4 3 ♘xd4 ♗xd4 4 ♗xd4 ♕xd4 5 ♘c2 ♕d3 6 ♘e3 isn't more than equality.

White might also look at 1 ... c5 since 2 dxc5 is virtually forced and 2 ... ♘xc3 3 dxc3 leaves White's pawns in a mess. But there's nothing convincing after that.

Black still shouldn't stop. If you look further and tweak this idea, it leads to the best move, **1 ... e3!**, with the idea of weakening the kingside. The game went **2 fxe3 c5! 3 dxc5 ♘xc3 4 bxc3 ♕xd2!**.

White to play

Black was winning (5 ♖f2 ♕xc3 or 5 ♘b5 ♘g4! 6 ♘f3 ♕xe3+ 7 ♔h1 ♘f2+.)

Better was 2 ♘f3! but Black holds an edge after 2 ... c5! 3 dxc5 ♘xc3 4 dxc3 ♘g4.

24. Black should be thinking that he has his own winning chances because g2 is vulnerable. For example **1 ... h4!** 2 ♖xg6 ♕xg6 and White must give up a piece to stop mate ... ♕xg2 mate. (He would be lost after 3 ♗g3 hxg3 4 ♕xg3 ♕xg3 5 fxg3 ♔g6 and ... ♔f5-e4.)

White kept the game alive with **2 ♖g4! ♖xg4 3 hxg4** but Black should keep his eye on mate and avoid 3 ... ♕d1+ 4 ♔h2 ♕xg4 in favor of **4 ... ♕f1!**.

Then on the forced **5 f3**:

Black to play

Black grabbed all the kingside pawns and won with **5 ... h3! 6 ♔xh3 ♗xf3 7 ♔g3 ♕xg2+**.

Better was 7 ♔h4 ♕xg2 8 ♕c8. But Black can still play to win with 8 ... f6! (9 ♕f5+ g6).

25. Black shouldn't try to equalize when he can be superior after **1 ... f5!**. That stops ♘e4, threatens ... f4 and begins an initiative.

The game went **2 ♘f3 ♘e5! 3 ♘xe5 ♗xe5** and he threatened 4 ... f4! 5 ♗d2 f3.

White tried for counterplay by going after the only target with **4 ♕b5.** But he was lost after **4 ... f4! 5 ♗xc5? ♖f5!**, threatening 6 ... f3 as well as the win of the White bishop thanks to a pin on the fourth rank.

For example, 6 ♗a3 f3 7 g3 ♗d4! and the attack prevails.

In the game Black won a piece after **6 f3 ♗f6! 7 d4 b6**. He could also have played 6 ... ♗d4 7 ♗xd4 ♖xb5. But, of course, he wanted *more*.

26. Time favors Black and his extra pawn. He has no immediate counterplay but can offer trades (... ♗b4, ... ♖ad8). Therefore White should attack and best is **1 g4!** to explode the kingside with 2 g5 hxg5 3 h6.

For example, 1 ... ♗b4 2 ♗xb4 ♕xb4 3 g5! hxg5 4 h6! ♕f4 5 h7+! ♘xh7 6 ♕h5 and wins. Or 4 ... ♕e7 5 h7+ ♔h8 6 ♖d7! ♘xd7 7 ♘xf7+.

The game actually went **1 ... ♗f8 2 g5! hxg5 3 h6! ♖e7** (3 ... ♕c7 4 ♖d7!) **4 hxg7 ♗xg7 5 ♘c4 resigns** in view of 5 ... ♕-moves 6 ♕xf6! and mates.

27. White played **1 ♔a1!**. Although the king seems safe on b1, he had two reasons to spend a tempo on another security move.

First, if White's queen leaves the second rank, which seems likely if his kingside attack gains speed, he wants to move his knight from c3 – such as to d5 – without allowing ... ♕xc2 with check.

In addition, he safeguards against ... ♘c4-a3 with check. For example, 1 ♘d4 ♘bc4 2 ♗xc4 ♘xc4 3 ♕d3 and now 3 ... ♕b6! is strong because 4 ♗c1? allows 4 ... ♘a3+ 5 ♔a1 ♕xd4! 6 ♕xd4 ♘xc2+ and ... ♘xd4.

In the game, Black found nothing better after 1 ♔a1! than **1 ... ♗f8**, after which **2 ♘d4!** was strong. The difference is that 2 ... ♘ec4 3 ♗xc4 ♘xc4 4 ♕d3 ♕b6 5 ♗c1! and the attack rolls on. (In the game, Black preferred **2 ... ♕c5** but after **3 g6!** White won.)

28. Black can win with ... ♖h6 followed by ... f4 and ... ♖eh5, to set up a mating combination with ... ♕xh2+!

That takes some preparation since a premature ... f4 allowed gxf4 with check.

White's pieces are so restrained that Black could take her time, even if she wasted time:

1 ... ♔f7! 2 ♕c2 ♖g6 3 ♕b1 ♔e7 4 ♕c2 ♔d8 5 ♕c1 ♔c8 6 ♕c2 ♔b8 7 ♕c1 ♔a7 8 ♕b1 ♔b8?! 9 ♕c2 ♖h6! 10 ♕c1 ♔a8 11 ♕d2 f4!.

White to play

Now 12 gxf4 ♖eh5 threatens 13 ... ♕xh2+ 14 ♘xh2 ♖xh2 mate. **White resigned** after **12 g4 ♖g5** in view of ... ♖xg4.

29. The only way to try to exploit White's lead in development is tactically. That means **1 ♘xd4! exd4 2 e5!**.

The first point is that 2 ... dxe5 3 ♗xb7 favors White (3 ... ♖b8 4 ♗c6+). The second is that 2 ... ♗xg2 3 exf6 ♗b7 allows White a clearly superior endgame with 4 fxe7 ♕xe7 5 ♕xe7+ ♔xe7 6 b3 and ♗a3.

30. If he can castle and find a good square for his bishop, Black will have the better game. White needs to act now and his most promising is **1 b4!**, to create a queenside target.

After **1 ... cxb4 2 ♘a4** he has strong chances, e.g. 2 ... ♕c7 3 ♖e1+ ♘e7 4 ♗f4 or 3 ... ♗e7 4 ♗b2 followed by ♖c1 and ♕d4.

The game went **2 ... ♕b5** and now both 3 ♗b2 ♘e7 4 ♖e1 and 3 ♗e3 ♘f6 4 ♘b6 and 5 a4 are promising.

31. The trend is running against White because Black has threats of ... ♕xf2 and ... ♖h5. If White defends with routine moves, such as 1 ♗f1 ♖h5 2 h3, Black will increase the pressure, e.g. 2 ... c5.

White chose **1 f4!**, which stops ... ♖h5, and halts the trend after **1 ... ♕xf2 2 ♗g4!**.

To maintain his extra pawn Black had to play **2 ... ♕xc2 3 ♖xc2 f5** but then came **4 ♗f3 ♖d7 5 ♖dc1**, with enough pressure to reach a drawable endgame (5 ... ♘d5 6 ♗xd5+ ♖xd5 7 ♖xc7).

32. No. As dominating as Black's pieces are, he can't win. He lacks a 'how'.

He might win if he could trade rooks or queens. But he can't force a swap. Nor can he effectively target f2, advance his king or push his kingside pawns. The game was drawn after 25 more moves but the outcome was clear after **1 ... ♕b3 2 ♔g2 ♕d5+ 3 ♔h2 ♕b3 4 ♔g2 ♕d5+ 5 ♔h2**.

33. Yes. White last move, **1 a4??**, made a win possible with **1 ... ♕xe4 2 fxe4 ♖xf2**.

Then 3 ♗xf2 ♖f3 is bad and the game continuation, **3 ♖xf2 ♖xf2 4 ♔xf2 a5!**, was worse because Black wins the a-pawn.

The win became obvious after **5 ♔e2 ♘c8 6 ♔d3 ♘b6 7 h4 ♘xa4 8 ♗c1 ♘b6 9 g4 ♔f7 10 ♗d2 a4 11 ♗c1 ♔f6 12 ♗a3 g5! 13 h5 ♔e7 14 ♗c1 ♘d7 15 ♔e2 ♘f6 16 ♔f3 ♔d7!** and the king will support ... b5 to gain entry to the queenside.

34. They are on the kingside. Black doesn't have enough king protection and this is revealed by **1 ♗xc6! bxc6 2 ♖d4!**, which threatens 3 ♖h4 ♖h8 4 ♕h6+ among other things.

Black gained some defensive space with **2 ... f5** but that exposed his second rank to **3 ♕d1!** and ♖d7.

Although Black could still resist with **3 ... ♔g6 4 ♖d7 ♕c5** this is the kind of position that shouldn't be holdable in the long run.

White to play

White could have won by getting his queen to e5, e.g. 5 ♕e1 ♔f6 6 b4 and 7 ♕a1+ or 5 ... ♖e8 6 b4! ♕c4 7 ♕e5 and wins.

Instead, he played **5 h4** to create the possibility of ♕d2-g5 mate or h4-h5+. The end was **5 ... ♖g8 6 ♕e1 ♔f6 7 ♔g2 ♖g4 8 ♕d2! ♕b4 9 ♕h6+ ♔e5 10 f4+ resigns**.

35. Trying to keep White's extra pawn with 1 ♕e2 allows Black a lot of pieces activity with 1 ... ♕e4 followed by ... ♖b3 or ... e5.

If White puts the queen on a more aggressive square, such as ♕d7, he prepares to push the c-pawn (1 ... ♖xb2? 2 c6).

But 1 ♕d7 is dubious because of 1 ... ♕e4 2 ♔f2 ♗f6, when Black prepares 3 ... ♖d8 as well as 3 ... ♗h4+.

The right way is **1 ♕c4!**. That stops both ... ♖b3 and ... ♕e4 and threatens to make the win trivially easy with 2 b4 or 2 c6.

The game went **1 ... ♕a1+ 2 ♔f2 ♖xb2 3 c6! ♖xd2+ 4 ♗xd2**, threatening 5 c7.

Black blockaded with **4 ... ♕a7+ 5 ♔e2 ♕c7** but was lost after **6 ♗a5!**.

201

Black to play

The pawn would queen after 6 ... ♕xa5 7 c7 ♕h5+ 8 ♔f2 ♕h4+ 9 ♔f1.

The game went **6 ... ♕c8 7 c7!** ♗**f8 8 ♕c6** and White 'wins in one move' – king to b6 – to prepare the blockade-breaking ♕b7!.

36. He should first look at **1 ♖d5**, not 1 ♖xf7 or even 1 bxa5. The reason is that **1 ... ♖xd5 2 exd5** is forced and the endgame may be a simple win. White's king can create a second passed pawn and it's only a matter of counting to see if it wins the race against Black's kingside pawns.

The game went **2 ... ♔g6 3 bxa5 bxa5 4 ♔d3 ♔f6 5 ♔c4 ♔e7** (not 5 ... ♔e5 6 ♔c5 and 7 d6).

White won the a-pawn, **6 ♔b5 ♔d6 7 ♔xa5** and then **7 ... f5 8 ♔b5 ♔xd5 9 a4 g5 10 a5 ♔d6**. White can't force the a-pawn through in time (11 ♔b6 f4). But the a-pawn will deflect the Black king, allowing White to win on the kingside: **11 ♔c4 ♔c6 12 ♔d4 ♔b5 13 ♔e5 f4 14 gxf4 gxf4 15 ♔xf4 ♔xa5 16 ♔g4** and White has a tempo more than he needs to win.

37. Not with 1 ♖xb7? ♖xb7 2 ♗xb7 because after 2 ... a5 and ... ♖xe7 he would have to work very hard to promote a queenside pawn.

Much easier is advancing his queenside pawns before taking on b7. The game went **1 b4! ♖xe7 2 ♖xe7 ♘xe7 3 a4!**.

Black to play

The pawns at a6 and b7 aren't going to escape. White will play a4-a5 and then take on b7, after which it should be easy to create a winning passer.

In the game Black saw how hopeless passive defense is and tried **3 ... ♖c8 4 ♗xb7 ♖c1+ 5 ♔g2 ♘f5**. But he could have resigned after **6 ♔f3 ♖c3+ 7 ♔e4 a5!? 8 bxa5 ♖c4+ 9 ♔d5 ♖xa4 10 a6**.

38. White wants to escape into an end game with **♕g3+**. But **1 ... ♔a8!** leaves him with both a difficult position and hard choices.

The post-mortem showed that **2 ♖g2 ♕h1+ 3 ♖g1 ♕h4** was the best, if unappetizing, try. Instead he chose **2 ♖g3? ♖c8!** and was lost, e.g. 3 ♖h3 ♖c1+! Or 3 ♔e1 ♕h1+ 4 ♔d2 ♕c1 mate.

The game ended with **3 ♖g2 ♕h1+ 4 ♖g1 ♕h4 5 ♖g2 ♖f3! 6 ♕d2** (6 ♕xf3 ♕h1+) **♕h1+ 7 ♖g1 ♕h3+** and **White resigned** before 8 ... ♖xd3.

39. With **1 ♖xc6!** and **1 ... bxc6 2 ♘xd4** he ensures that his next several moves will be easier to find than Black's.

This comes at a small material cost and with the compensation of Black's wrecked queenside pawns and his weakness on light squares. That is clear after, say, 2 ... c5 3 ♘xf5 ♕xf5 4 ♘e4.

The game went **2 ... ♘b8 3 ♘xf5 ♕xf5 4 ♘e4** and Black was forced to make tough choices.

Black to play

He made the wrong ones, **4 ... ♘d7?** (4 ... ♕e5) **5 ♖xc6 ♘e5 6 ♖c5** and **6 ... ♘f3+?!** (6 ... ♕h5!). He was losing soon after **7 ♔h1 ♕g6 8 ♖xa5**.

40. Black has a choice between giving White a strong initiative (with 1 ... dxc5 or 1 ... ♗xc3) or seizing his own. White felt that 1 ... ♗xc3 would have been second-best because he has a powerful position after either 2 ♗xc3 dxc5 3 e5 ♘d7 4 0-0 and 5 f5 or 2 ♖xc3 dxc5 3 e5 ♘d7 4 0-0 0-0 5 ♖g3.

He praised his opponent's **1 ... 0-0!** even though 2 cxd6 ♕xd6 3 e5 costs a piece. It turns out that Black has his own initiative – and much easier moves to find – after play went **3 ... ♕d8 4 exf6 ♖e8**.

White to play

Now 5 ♗e3 ♕xf6! (6 0-0? ♖xe3! or 6 ♔f1 ♗g4!) is dubious and 5 ♘e4 ♗f5 6 ♖c4 ♖c8 or 6 ♗xa5 ♕xa5+ 7 ♔f2 ♕b6+ was risky. The game was eventually drawn.

41. With **1 ... ♗xc2!** and a bit of calculation, Black reduced the results to two. It should be easy to see that 2 ♖c4 ♕xc4 3 ♗xc4 ♗xd1 can end only in a Black win or a draw. (A win is more likely.)

The more complex alternative is **2 ♖c1! ♖b1!** based on 3 ♖xb1 ♗xd3 and 3 ♖c4 ♕d8! (4 ♕xd8 ♖xd8 5 ♖xb1 ♗xb1 6 ♗xb1 ♖d1+).

White improves with **3 ♖ee1!**:

Black to play

But once again Black has a simple way to secure two results: **3 ... ♗xd3! 4 ♖xc7 ♖xe1+** with a rook, bishop and pawn for the queen, and all the pawns on the kingside. It was drawn in 15 more moves.

42. "Where did I err?" White asked after Black gave up the bishop and won. "After all, the sacrifice could hardly be correct," he insisted.

This was a conventional attitude more than 60 years ago. There was no forced win after **3 hxg3 ♕xg3+** since White avoided 4 ♔h1 0-0 5 fxe4? ♘g4!. Black only gets two pawns for his piece.

But 14-year-old Boris Spassky was polite enough not to tell his elder opponent that Black's initiative almost certainly justified the sacrifice, even after **4 ♘g2! ♗h3**.

The post-mortem showed that after **5 ♖f2 0-0**, Black does well in the complications of **6 ♗xh6 ♖xf3**.

Instead, the game went **5 ♕e2 0-0 6 ♕f2**.

Black to play

It's the initiative that matters, and that's why Black rejected 6 ... ♕xf3? 7 ♗xh6! and 6 ... ♖xf3 7 ♕xg3 ♖xg3 8 ♔h2, when his pressure is over.

Instead, **6 ... ♕g6!** led to a quick win just by adding more pieces to the kingside – **7 ♗e2 ♖f6 8 f4 ♘f5 9 ♔h2 ♕h6 10 ♖h1 ♗xg2+** and **White resigned** in light of 11 ♔xg2 ♖g6+.

43. 1 ♕e2? is a mistake because it allowed a 'must-be-sound' sacrifice, **1 ... ♖d4! 2 exd4 ♘d5**. Black may have looked no further than to see that he threatens ... ♘xf4 and that after **3 ♕d2** he can continue **3 ... ♘ac7**.

White to play

Black was certain of his compensation because the f4-pawn will fall, after ... ♘e6 or ... ♕h5-h4. He could also see that neither of White's rooks was as good as Black's d5-knight. (In fact, White tried to give material back immediately with **4 ♖fe1 ♖e8 5 ♖e3!?** – which Black ignored with **5 ... ♘xf4!**.)

He had a commanding position and won after **6 ♗f1 ♕f6 7 ♗c4+ ♔f8 8 ♔h1 ♘cd5 9 ♗xd5 ♘xd5 10 ♖h3 h6 11 ♖g1 f4 12 ♕d1 f3 13 ♖hg3 g5 14 ♕d2 ♘f4**.

44. Both 1 ... ♗xd4 and 1 ... ♘xd4 give Black two pawns but nothing more. Black improved his piece coordination with **1 ... ♖e7** instead.

White blundered with **2 g3?**, which made **2 ... ♗xd4! 3 exd4 ♘xd4 4 ♕a4 ♘f3+ 5 ♔h1 ♘xe1** into a very favorable sacrifice. Black's central pawns tip the positional balance in his favor after **6 ♘xe1 d4** and **7 ... c5**.

45. 1 ♖e4 allows Black to make a promising sacrifice, 1 ... dxc3! 2 ♖xg4 ♖xd3 3 cxd3 cxb2 4 ♖b1 ♗xa3.

Much better for White is **1 ♗b4!**, which gave him a strong attack after **1 ... ♗xb4 2 axb4 ♘xb4 3 ♕c4**. Black was in trouble after **3 ... ♘c6 4 b4**.

Black to play

White threatens 5 b5 ♘-moves 6 ♖xa7, with a quick win. Black didn't like 4 ... a6 in view of the line-opening 5 b5 axb5 6 ♕xb5 or simply 5 ♖xa6!, which is complicated but works.

The game ended with **4 ... ♔b8 5 b5! ♘xe5 6 ♘xe5 fxe5** and now **7 ♖xa7! Resigns**. It's mate after 7 ... ♔xa7 8 ♕xc7 and ♖a1.

46. Since 1 ♗h4 ♕-moves 2 ♗f6 wins the Exchange, the only question is whether Black has compensation in that line or after the alternative, the queen sacrifice 1 ... ♕xh4 2 ♖h2.

It doesn't take long to determine that Black gets no positional plusses if he surrenders the Exchange. But his rooks are able to seize the initiative after **1 ... ♕xh4! 2 ♖h2 ♖h7 3 ♖xh4 ♖xh4**.

White to play

The rooks can make progress with ... ♖fh7, ... ♖h3 and ... ♖7h4. But even if they couldn't do anything offensive and were limited to maintaining control of the h-file, Black would have more than enough comp.

In the game White correctly tried to complicate after **4 ♕e2 ♖fh7 5 ♕g2 ♖h3!** with **6 f5!**. He managed to draw, with some luck.

47. Yes, he has comp. If White defends against ... ♗xg4, Black gets good play (1 ♘h2 ♗d7 and ... ♗a4 or 1 g5 ♗f5).

White's antidote was **1 ♖d4!** so that **1 ... ♗xd4 2 cxd4** gives him excellent compensation of his own (2 ... ♘d7 3 ♗xh6 ♖e8 4 ♗d3 with the idea of ♗xg6).

Black tried **2 ... ♘a6** instead and White won after **3 ♘e5 ♖d8 4 ♕d2** (threat of ♕xh6) **♕f8 5 ♗c4** and **6 d6**.

48. White would have solid positional compensation if he's allowed to play g2-g4 and establish an unassailable knight on d4.

Black's best is **1 ... d4!**. Even though it increases White's material compensation, it reduces his positional plusses. Now 2 g4 ♘e3 or 2 ... ♖fd8! 3 gxf5 d3 and ... ♕xb5 is good for Black.

White played **2 ♘bxd4 ♘xd4 3 ♘xd4** and Black had the edge after **3 ... ♖c3 4 ♔h2 ♖fc8**.

All of his pieces are working (... ♕d5, ... ♖c1) and the game ended abruptly after one mistake, **5 ♕b2?**, which allowed Black to win with **5 ... ♕e4! 6 ♔g1 ♖c2! 7 ♘xc2 ♖xc2** (8 ♕b1 ♗c5).

49. The pawn structure indicates it's on the kingside. That suggests **1 ... f5!** is right. It makes his light square bishop bad but what matters more is ... f4.

Since 2 g3 f4! 3 gxf4 ♗e4 walks into trouble, play went **2 bxc6 bxc6 3 ♖ac1 ♗e8 4 ♕a6 ♗d7** and when White failed to play 5 g3 he quickly went downhill:

5 ♗c3? f4! 6 exf4 ♖xf4 7 ♖ce1 ♗d6 8 ♗b5 ♕f7 9 ♗a4 (9 ♗xc6 ♖f6! 10 ♗xd7 ♗xh2+) **♖f8 10 ♖e2? ♖h4!** and **Black won**.

50. It's a very good structure but it can be exploited only by a priyome that targets the light square weaknesses in Black's camp, h7, f7 and e6.

In previous games, White relied on normal development, such as 1 ♗g5 ♘ge7 2 ♖c1, and got no advantage.

Instead, he has to rearrange his minor pieces, ♗d3 and ♘e2-f4, so they prepare ♕c2 and/or ♘g5, with an attack on h7 and e6.

This time White had a clear advantage following **1 ♗d3! ♘ge7 2 ♘e2! ♖c8 3 ♘f4** and then **3 ... ♕b6 4 a3 a5 5 ♖b1** and ♘g5.

51. White wants to change it with c3-c4, since ... dxc4/♗xc4 would give him play for his bishops and ... d4 offers him chances after f3-f4 and ♗g2.

Black played **1 ... c4!**, which not only makes his bishop a bit better but sharply limits White's pieces. After **2 f4 g6!** he had stopped the liberating idea of 3 f5 exf5 4 e6 and assured himself the superior game.

52. The sacrificial priyome is **1 fxe6 fxe6 2 e5!**, another device designed to clear e4 for the knight (2 ... fxe5 3 ♘e4 and wins). Here it's based on lines such as 2 ... d5 3 ♘e4 dxe4? 4 ♕xd7 mate.

Black avoided immediate disaster with **2 ... ♕xe5** but White obtained a powerful initiative with **3 ♖he1 ♕g5 4 ♕d4!**, renewing the threat of ♘e4. He eventually won after **4 ... 0-0-0 5 ♕a7 ♕c5 6 ♕xa6+ ♔b8 7 ♗xe6**.